To Auntie Ch
Lenee
Dawn
xx

Slowly Making Ripples

Slowly Making Ripples

By Dawn Faizey Webster

ISBN 978-1-4457-5206-8

For Alexander and my family as without their love and support

I would never have survived.

Chapter 1

On 9th June 2003 the alarm bells rang. I called in at my GP to see a midwife, as my ankle was a little bit swollen and I was going to work so I thought I had better get a check-up. The midwife immediately called for an ambulance because my blood pressure was high and I had protein in my urine. I was sent to Stafford Hospital with lights flashing and the siren going. When I arrived they said my baby would have to be delivered immediately, but the hospital was not equipped to cope with such a small baby. I was only twenty-six weeks into my pregnancy. I was again put into an ambulance and with lights flashing and sirens going and transferred to the city hospital in Stoke on Trent.

At 2.15 a.m. on the 15th June 2003 Alexander Simon Thomas Webster was born by Caesarean section, weighing one pound, eight ounces and eleven inches long, less than a bag of sugar. I saw him briefly and heard him cry before he was whisked off to the special care baby unit alias 'neo-natal'. I had been told that this would happen, so I was expecting it.

I then remember the surgeon discussing with his colleague about doing the 'Cornish pasty' stitch. I said I wasn't too keen on being sewn up like a Cornish pasty! I was then taken to a recovery room and my parents and my husband Simon came in to see me. I was starving hungry and thirsty so it was agreed I could have some tea and toast. I stayed in recovery until the epidural had worn off and then was moved back to the high dependency unit. As expected, I was extremely tired but the Adrenalin was still flowing, so there was no way I could sleep. That night I was given a Morphine injection as a painkiller which gave me weird dreams.

On the afternoon of the next day I was sent back up to the ward but now as a post-natal patient. Each day my blood pressure was checked but it still wasn't coming down and I still had the pain in my neck that had started a couple of days earlier. This pain was a result of me cricking my neck while I was asleep, according to the doctor. One night while driving home after visiting me, Simon hit a black dog, now I'm not particularly superstitious but a black dog is supposed to be a particularly bad omen and in this case it was, the events following this incident verify this fact.

Simon had been able to see Alexander on the day he was born but due to my weakened state I could not see him properly until the next day, I was nervous seeing him at first because of all the tubes and wires, but as soon as I saw the tiny creature in the incubator I was filled with love. I went down to see him every morning and every night and the nurses advised me to start expressing my milk as soon as possible. I used a breast pump and took the bottles down with me. Because he was so premature, Alexander was only given a tiny drop of milk so the rest was frozen for future use. My blood pressure still hadn't improved; I was on two types of medication, which only succeeded in keeping it stable.

My mind was in turmoil as I really wanted to go home but I didn't want to leave my baby behind. On the Thursday it was suggested that I might go home but a doctor needed to see me first so one was found. I hadn't seen him before and after looking at my blood test results and my blood pressure he decided that it was to soon for me to leave, I was very disappointed as I had built my hopes up and I really wanted to go home, perhaps someone should have explained to me just how ill I was. Again the next day I was assessed to go home, this time by a doctor I knew. He said that my blood pressure would eventually go back to normal so I could leave the hospital. I gathered my things and helped by Simon, took them out to the car, I then went back to see Alexander before going home. Simon didn't come with me as he said he wasn't going all the way out to the car and then having to come back into the hospital.

When I got home I immediately phoned my parents to tell them I was back and to ask them to come round, because a friend of mine was coming to see me. Simon went to fetch fish and chips for my tea as that was what I really fancied. After tea my parents and my friend arrived. At first we made general conversation but then talk turned to visiting Alexander. I said I would visit him every day but Simon chipped in that we may not be able to afford it. I stated that as I am Alexander's mother and due to his importance to me, I would go every day regardless of the cost. Simon replied, "Oh no you won't." This outburst made the room go silent and after my friend left I burst into tears, I just wanted my baby home!

Each morning I phoned the neo-natal unit to see how Alexander was and each evening we visited him. After a few days I couldn't bear to make the morning call so Simon did it for me. On the Wednesday Simon received a speeding fine as he had been previously caught on a camera coming to visit me in hospital, and he went ballistic. I thought at the time that this isn't helping my blood pressure. He had also decided with rather odd timing to change his motorbike from something sensible for touring, to something sporty. He made that his priority, so visiting Alexander could wait. My parents therefore took me to see Alexander because I was too dizzy to drive myself. From that Wednesday onwards I started to have more dizzy spells, mild at first but they quickly started to become stronger as I couldn't focus and my head felt like lead. I still had a pain in my neck.

Whilst visiting Alexander in the neo-natal unit on Thursday, I fainted. On Friday I mentioned how I had been feeling to the visiting midwife who said it was due to blood loss during the Caesarean. She said I needed iron tablets so she phoned the surgery for a prescription. As I was lying on the settee just after she had left, I had what I can only describe as a 'funny turn'. I felt as though I was dreaming but I was actually awake, I also had split-level sight as my right eye saw everything distorted and higher than my left eye.

Chapter 2

I awoke the next morning feeling worse than ever. I had pins and needles down my right side and my speech was slurred. It was 5.45 a.m.

Simons was up and ready to go out. He said he would phone my parents. I heard him on the phone saying, "I have, but there is not one on duty," "I can't unfortunately, I am going out." When he came back into the bedroom he told me he had informed my mother that he had phoned a doctor although I never heard him do that. He said he would stay with me but I told him to go. My parents came straight away. They only lived a few minutes away. My mother took one look at me and dialled 999. It was obvious I'd had a stroke. My mother cleaned me up as I was frothing at the mouth, and put a clean nightdress on me. By this time the ambulance was at the door and I was taken to Stafford A&E.

When I arrived at A & E I was put into a cubicle to wait for the doctor. My mother came in and then a nursing Sister who asked a lot of questions, which my mother answered most of as I found it difficult to speak – I had all this foam in my mouth and could not swallow very well. My mother emphasised that I was experiencing a lot of pain in the back of my neck. A doctor came in to take some blood which I prefer to keep in my body as it is at home there. He could not find a vein so he decided to take it from my groin but I was dying to go to the toilet. I forgot to mention that the doctor who was trying to take my blood was losing enough of his own; he had a nose bleed, which he wiped on the back of his glove!

My mother asked for a bedpan for me, but the doctor said he wanted to take my blood first. Luckily my Mom saw the nice Irish

Sister that had been with me when I first came in and asked her for a bedpan. She immediately pushed the doctor away from the bed and got me a bedpan (phew, what a relief!) The doctor then came back in to take my blood, which hurt a lot. He had a little white plaster on his nose but I noticed he had not changed his gloves; I could still see blood on the back of them. I then saw another doctor who told me I needed to have a CT scan. My mother asked if there was something they could give me for the terrible pain in my neck, but the doctor said 'no' as they did not know what they were treating.

I eventually went for the CT scan around lunchtime. My parents had to leave me while I went. My mum phoned Simon – I asked her to as I thought he would be back by then. I would not tell her where he had gone. But she got no answer. She also phoned my brother Mark and his wife Helen. By the time I had had my scan, they were both waiting to see me. I asked Mark and Helen to go to see Alexander, as I was worried about him.

The scan showed no bleeding so the doctor said they would do another scan the next day. I was then transferred to a ward and given a lumbar puncture.

My mum and dad went back home to get me some toiletries and nightwear and also to find out what had happened to Simon. I was a little worried, as I knew where he had gone. It was around 4 p.m. by this time. I think all hell let loose when my mother drove up the drive and saw Simon polishing the brand new motorbike he had gone to collect that morning. Eventually he turned up at the hospital.

I was put on a drip and blood pressure machine. Simon and my family stayed until visiting time was over. As the evening wore on I started to feel quite ill. I told the nurse then I remember no more. I lost consciousness. Later I was told that the doctor did not know what to do, it was at 10 p.m. They phoned my brother (for some reason he was down as my next of kin) at 12 midnight to say I had deteriorated.

When my family arrived, the doctor said they had phoned a neurologist to ask for advice but he was in theatre. The advice finally came through at 2 a.m. and I was put on Heparin at 4 a.m. I remember coming round with Mark at my side. He was saying, "Squeeze my hand if you can," which I was able to do. Then my mother was there and I lifted my left arm and pointed to my neck which was still painful. I could not speak. Funnily, I don't remember Simon being there. I was told, a year later, that Simon *was* there but when asked if he would stay the night with me as I was so ill, said he had got to go home to feed the cat. (I think it was more to check his new bike was safe).Mark stayed with me for the night. I was then transferred to North Staffordshire hospital, Multiple Injuries Unit the following day, but by the time I got there, I was again unconscious. I knew no more for about a week as I drifted in and out of consciousness.

After my brother had sat with me all night he had a sort of epiphany and followed a secretly harboured ambition to become a nurse, he is now a fully qualified community nurse. I remember my sister-in-law Helen talking to me and she promised to buy me some pink boots when I was able to wear them (I am going to keep her to that promise).

The hospital staff told my husband and family to bring in CDs of books that I liked and also pictures that I might recognise. Simon brought in a photo of a holiday we'd had in Egypt with a large photo of Tutankhamen. I vaguely remember seeing the photos but the CDs (Oh no!): I had earphones put in my ears and they played Michael Palin's trek across the desert. Then they played it again and again, not knowing that I was conscious more than unconscious. They would never let it run to the end and I had the beginning and middle bits over and over again. The mere mention of Michael Palin's name now and I shudder!

I had a tracheotomy tube put in just after I arrived at the MIU. It is a tube put into your neck and it is then attached to an oxygen cylinder to help you breathe. I was later to find out how hard it was to get it removed. I also apparently, when a nurse said she was going to clean my teeth, clamped my mouth shut and it took a year before anyone decided to do something about opening it, (which eventually they did) I could open the left side about an inch and was fed through a tube which went up my nose.

The nurses moved my bed from one end of the ward to the other end by a door. I could hear the traffic going by. On my left side was a young Indian man who had been in a car accident and he screamed and thrashed about a lot. His young wife and mother were so distressed. I could only look on with pity.

I was obviously drifting in and out of consciousness all the time, initially being more unconscious than conscious with some strange dreams as a consequence. The earliest one I can remember involved being on a conveyer belt having just had Alexander, and hanging in front of me was his birth certificate. All I had to do was grab it to go home but I could only stare at it. Another one that I recall was where I needed to be cryogenically frozen to get home, but I could not get cold enough! In some instances I was obviously semiconscious as I was aware that a nurse washed my hair while I was an Iraqi soldier (it does make you wonder what drugs they were giving me!).

As things started to feel increasingly real when in a semiconscious state, it became important to me to be able to tell when I was fully conscious. I found that I could use the cards by my bed as a gauge, only when fully conscious were they there.

I was fully awake now but no one knew. I simply lay there. I was paralysed. I could move nothing except my eyes. Simon and my family would come every day. They would talk to me, talk to each other and to the nurses but I could do nothing to let them know I knew what was going on. I lay there wondering what I was going to do.

The nurses took my wedding ring off and gave it to Simon and then they cut the toe ring off my second to big toe. What were they getting me ready for?

After two weeks I was transferred to a High Dependency Unit. In HDU I was in a great deal of pain with my legs but I could tell none of the nurses about it. I just had to lie there and bear it. I remember thinking how can my face not convey the pain I am in; surely I was pale and sweaty. The one thing I always enjoyed was the rain, of which there is plenty in Stoke-On-Trent, as I found the noise of it on the window so soothing.

By this time I was fully conscious most of the day yet the highly scientific method of detecting this that the doctors were using failed. It did not occur to them that actually I simply could not squeeze their hand to let them know I wasn't unconscious.

Then one day Mark and Dad were with me. The hospital rule was only two people could be at a bed at any time. My mother used to come in with Simon. Mark said to Dad, "I am sure she can hear us." (brilliant Mark!) He took my hand and said, "Dawn, if you can hear me, will you blink your eyes." I blinked. Dad went mad, running from the ward shouting, "She has blinked to say yes." My communication had started. A few days earlier Simon had said to the doctors that he thought I was reading the book he was holding, which I was, but they pooh-poohed it as they said I would not be out of my coma properly for some months.

My family started to use the alphabet to get me to spell out what I wanted to say; when they reached the letter I wanted I simply looked up, the first word I spelt out as a test was dog. It took ages, as they would start at A and go through the alphabet every time.

The first question I asked Mark so he advised me later was, "Am I going to die?" Then my sister-in-law Helen, who is a teacher, came to visit me and she had devised a letter board. She had separated the alphabet into four squares so all anyone had to do was point to a square and say those letters. It worked very well and I no longer felt cut off from everyone.

The first thing I spelt out to Simon was: "Will you wait for me?" He did not answer me. Another time I asked Simon to kill me but all he said was, "No, I will get into trouble" – no word of comfort I also asked my mother to look after Simon for me, which she promised to do but that was short-lived because Simon's behaviour became unreasonable.

Chapter 3

The doctors tried to wean me off oxygen and also get my tracheotomy tube out if possible. On the day they were going to try I was unexpectedly moved to Ward 24, a neurological ward. I had been moved to the High Dependency Unit two weeks earlier. I was to stay in this ward for five months. The staff were always nice to me (as they were in MIU and HDU) but in Ward 24 they talked to me knowing I could understand them, and some of them would use my letter board so I was able to tell them about the pain in my leg.

My first physiotherapy was given to me on Ward 24. One morning three physiotherapists came in and hoisted me out of my bed and put me on a tilt table. They put some strapping around me then stood me up. It was marvellous! I thought if they keep working on me I will soon be better, but this was not to be. There was a great shortage of physiotherapists, occupational therapists and Speech and Language staff. I was also not aware until much later that recovery from my type of stroke would take an extremely long time.

I therefore had physiotherapy sporadically. The OT would come in to show my parents what to do with my hands, how to stretch them and they made me some splints to keep my fingers straight, which I wore for at least four hours each day. I also had boots made for me which were like moon boots. They were to stop my feet from dropping.

Every day Simon and my parents went to see Alexander and reported back to me how he was. Then one of the neonatal nurses came up with a brilliant idea; all the nurses would keep a diary for me of what happened in Alexander's day-to-day activities. But the best thing of all was that it was done as if Alexander had written it himself.

It started with 'Dear Mummy' and saying if he had been a good boy and had drunk all of his milk or if he had been a bit naughty and wet on the nurse's hand. Alexander was still so tiny and very poorly.

One day I heard a commotion outside my door. Then the nurses came in and turned my bed so it was up against the wall. All they would say was "Don't worry, it's all right." The door opened again and in came an incubator and there was my Alexander! I was shocked. It was the most marvellous thing they could have done. He had wires all over his body. They plugged him in and lifted me up so I could lie looking at him. He was so tiny and my body was in such a mess but I felt I was so lucky to have him and I was so happy!

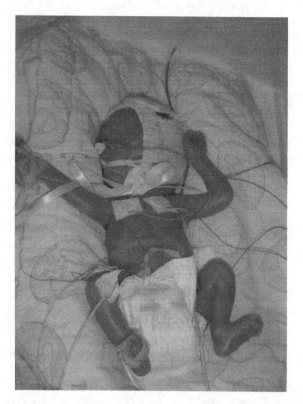

It had now been a month now since my stroke and Simon's attitude had changed toward my parents, and me. When he came to see me he was always so angry. He had started to worry about money – why, I don't know as I was still getting paid my full wages and he still got his wages.

We both had good jobs. I was an IT teacher at a private Grammar school in Stafford and he was the manager of the local Post Office delivery depot. The outgoing bills were minimal as my mother brought Simon's lunch to the hospital and most nights invited him back late at night for a cooked meal. Some of these were already prepared by my aunt.

Even so, Simon started to spend less time with me. When he came, he arrived late and left early. Then he would miss the odd weekend because he wanted to go off on his motorbike. This caused a great deal of argument between my mother and him. Simon said he had the right to live his own life, but my mother knew how much I wanted him to be with me. I would hope and pray he would stop thinking of himself and be there for Alexander and me because when he missed visiting me he also missed visiting Alexander.

One day Simon came in and was going mad because he wanted a letter from the hospital about my illness to give to the credit card company as he said I would get blacklisted. The hospital said that they would deal with them directly but Simon would not agree to it; he wanted the letter himself. I realise now it was for him to use for all his deceptions. My parents unknowingly eventually helped him obtain it.

Things finally came to a head one day when Simon said he wanted to re-mortgage our house. I said 'no' but as I could do nothing about it, he was going ahead. Simon had a sister in London who was going to organise it all. I talked it over with Mark and he offered to be my Power of Attorney if there was no way of stopping Simon from what he wanted to do. Simon got angry when I told him of Mark's suggestion. He wanted no help from my family at all. He then came in one day all smiles. He told me he had been practising my signature and he thought he had got it right. He then started to practise it again in front of my parents. My dad went mad when he realised what was happening. He threatened Simon with the police. Simon said **** off and my mother had to push my father out of the room. Simon then stormed off. It was some time later Simon told me he had actually re-mortgaged our property with the help of his sister.

My parents said no more about the mortgage and things drifted back to as normal as they could be between my parents and Simon. I had a few hiccoughs with the nurses inasmuch as a couple of them were somewhat thoughtless. One night a nurse took my blood. She leaned my arm on the cot side as she took it but then went away and left my arm there and I was unable to move it, I never slept that night or the next night when she did it again. My mother had a few strong words with her.

I was always turned on my sides, left to right and then back again. It was to help my lungs. One night I was turned but not positioned properly and when I coughed, I fell and hung over the side of the bed and there I stayed until they found me, I think it was about an hour later. From then on, I had a great fear of falling. Also I could not lie on my left side as then only my right eye and ear exposed and as they are both defunct I could not hear or see anything properly. Unfortunately a male nurse, who was a bit of a jobs worth, did just that while I watching *A Touch of Frost,* so to add insult to injury not only could I not see or hear properly but also the telly was now behind me!

I still had some wonderful nurses and care workers in this ward. They kept saying because of my strength in accepting the condition I was in, some of them look at life differently. I could not see the point of getting upset and having to have a lot of anti-depression tablets. I simply thought what had happened has happened and you cannot change the past. I had to look to the future and make my body work again.

Ward 24 was split into two groups. One side was called the red side; the other was the blue side. As I said, they had some lovely nurses and care workers. One nurse, if she was working on the opposite side to mine (I was on the red side) would come in and give me a kiss on the forehead, say "Hello," and run out again. Another care worker would come in and tell me a joke and say, "Don't tell it to your mother," then run out again.

I saw the funny side of the mishaps. There was one where the nurse was trying to change the tube in my nose that went down to my stomach to feed me. She was trying for ages to get it down and then she was all smiles because she thought she had succeeded but I spelt out "no, it is all in my mouth!" but after a few more attempts she was successful.

There were good days and bad days and it was funny but when I had a good day my parents would tell me that when they saw Alexander he'd had a good day but when Alexander had a bad day, so did I!

One day when Mark was with me he noticed my eye had got what he described as a crater on my cornea. He had noticed it before when I was in HDU although he had not mentioned it but now he said it looked worse. He informed the nurses and an ophthalmologist was sent for. It was my right eye – the main side of my stroke – and apparently it was because my eye did not fully close. The doctor wanted me to have my eye closed for a while by having a patch put over it, but I became very frightened. I could not move or speak and now they wanted to take half of my vision away no matter how distorted. There was, however, a compromise; I would have a patch put on only at night. Things went well for a while but then they decided it needed to close better in the day when I blinked. The main treatment decided upon was to lubricate it and a gold weight was put on to the lid to help it close. It was quite funny really. As the gold weight was only tiny it had to be stuck on with tape which kept coming unstuck, then there would be a search of the pillows for the gold weight!

After the doctors had made sure that a gold weight would work well, they decided to operate and insert the weight into my eyelid. I went to the theatre and had a local anaesthetic and I was amazed how they did it but the gold weight did what they hoped for.

I then had another surprise visit from Alexander. He came over in his incubator but he had fewer wires on him. The nurse decided to strip him of his clothes and tuck him down my nightdress. It was wonderful feeling his little naked body on mine. He lay there so contented. He had now started to improve and I felt at last he was going to make it.

Alexander started to make regular visits to me and I would watch Simon feed him. Oh how I longed to hold him and feed him but Simon never offered to help me do it. Then on one visit, the Polish nurse that brought him over just took him off Simon and she helped me to hold him. She put my hand around the bottle. Although she was actually doing the holding, it was so good to feel I was feeding him.

Things between Simon and my parents went up and down. If it was up, Simon would do something to upset me, like the time he brought videos of our holiday. They showed me running over fields, laughing, eating, drinking – all the things I could no longer do and it upset me greatly. My mother asked him to stop but he wouldn't. He said *he* wanted to see it even if I didn't. It never occurred to him to turn the TV away from me so I had to put up with it. I tried to close my eyes to most of it. Once, when he was in a bad mood, he sat in the corner. He had come in without saying a word and I was facing the opposite way so I could not see him. I asked my mother where Simon was, when she came in. She was very cross when she realised what he was doing.

I don't know what was happening to Simon. We had a good marriage. Ups and downs like anyone else but we got on well together. We were out most of the time, having meals at my parents' house. On odd occasions we would invite my parents for a meal. We had plenty of holidays. We always went abroad for our main holiday every year. Sometimes we had holidays in England with my parents. We had weekend breaks. Then we decided to have a baby and it was when I first went into hospital I think he changed. He was on his own and this was something he could not cope with. It never occurred to him that it was his behaviour that was causing all the arguments.

Simon's visits dropped down to just three quarters of an hour most week days, coming at eleven a.m. and going before my parents arrived at twelve noon. Simon started to tell his family that my parents would not let him have any quality time with me, yet when my mother rang him at my request to ask him to stay longer; he said unfortunately he could not as hospitals are dreary places. I settled down to accepting Simon's attitude and I hoped he might come to understand that I needed his support, as well as my family to help me through. It was really his support more than my parents that I wanted.

One day I heard the physiotherapists talking about a 'Swedish nose'. It is a nozzle which fits over a tracheotomy tube with a filter on each side. Apparently it is the next step to getting a tracheotomy tube out, but first you have to be able to breathe without having oxygen. I became obsessed with getting a Swedish nose. Every day I asked my parents if they could find out when I would have one and every day they would say, "When you are ready". One day, when I was having a bath, the nurse forgot to put me back on oxygen. (I have always felt she did it on purpose to help me) so she phoned the physiotherapists and asked what to do. They said if I had managed without oxygen for that length of time (I forget how long it was) then put a Swedish nose on me. I was over the moon! To me it was a giant step forward.

One weekend, Simon came rushing in his motorbike gear to say he had lost his key while out with some friend. He spoke to my parents to ask them for their key and as he had left his friend at our house, he was in a hurry. He took the key and left without even speaking or looking at me at all. Can you imagine the hurt inside I felt? I think the hurt I felt over the way he was treating me was harder to bear than my stroke. Also his temper was leading to bizarre behaviour, such as when his mother came down from Blackpool with his stepfather to the hospital to see her first grandchild and he told her that she could not see Alexander because he was too ill, despite the fact that my parents had just left him. His mother was extremely upset so my father said he would take her to see Alexander but she would not go because Simon had said no.

Ward 24 had only the one wheelchair. The nurses put me in it one day so my father asked if I could go out of my room. They said yes, so I went down to the day room. Although I was not expected to move anything for a long time, I felt that I could, or I would move my head. I practised, but I did not have the strength to move my head when it was on a pillow. They had to pad me around with pillows when I was in the wheelchair. Anyway, my father decided to put a board between my head and the pillow (it was a chess board), so that I had nothing to obstruct me from moving. It was great. I practised every time I could get in the wheelchair. One day, when I managed to be put in the wheelchair, my dad could not get the board because someone was playing chess, so I got my parents to wedge me against a wall so I could practise my turning. My head started to turn. It was better to the left than the right. I did not care. I was moving! Another achievement, I thought.

Another nice thing happened. Simon came in with a get well card from a friend I had met on the Internet a few years earlier. He lived in Scotland. I had met 'Stu' and his parents once when I was in Scotland. The card had the most wonderful words in it you could wish to read. Stu had written them about me. As he had not heard from me for some time, he had emailed Simon to ask if I was all right. He knew I was having a baby. He was so upset to hear of my stroke. Stu turned out to be my knight in shining armour in the years to come. I also had cards and gifts from many people, some from the school where I taught. A lot said 'Get Well Soon', I suppose it depends what they meant by 'Soon'.

I spent my 31st birthday and our 8th wedding anniversary in Ward 24. Little did I realise then that it would be the last time we would celebrate our anniversary.

I had a stream of visitors and as long as they used my letter board I could join in a conversation. Except on one occasion, when a lovely vicar visited. He was the chaplain at the hospital and was such an interesting conversationalist; I simply sat there in awe. He had different tales to tell every time he came, of his experiences abroad, his family, his love of food and how he cooked it. Religion never came into it except he gave me this lovely feeling of life.

Also whilst in Ward 24 my balance went and I felt constantly dizzy, it was like the spirit level in my head was malfunctioning. When I lay on my right side it felt like the room was sloping downward behind me and although I knew in reality that the room was flat, I still felt that I would slide off the bed if I did not hold on. Obviously the main problem was that I couldn't hold on and so I became increasingly tense and panicky. Lying on my back was not as bad, as my feet felt higher than my head. Then, gradually, the feeling and the dizziness subsided until they were no more.

One weekend, when Simon was out on his motorbike, he had a bad accident. My mother made light of it as she never wanted me to worry and so she told me that he had skidded off his motorbike and was fine but his motorbike was a mess so he was staying down in Cheltenham until he had got it fixed. I believed her, as I knew Simon would not leave his motorbike. The truth was that he was in hospital for a few days after hitting a car and going through the rear window and had his neck slashed. I was told the truth when he was out of hospital. They said it was a few millimetres from his jugular vein. My mother phoned his father in Gloucester a couple of times to find out how he was for me and unbelievably Simon told everyone when he came back that my parents had never bothered to enquire about him!

I eventually arrived at the top of the list for The Haywood Rehabilitation centre in Stoke. A lovely lady came to assess me but I failed because I had an NG tube up my nose to feed me and a tracheotomy tube in. She said that they may accept the tracheotomy but I would need to be fed through a PEG (Percutaneous Endoscopic Gastrostomy) That is a tube put in your stomach that you food is put through.

The new Registrar decided that he would send me to the outpatients department to have a PEG put in. I went and then I came back again! Nobody had mentioned to the doctor who was going to perform this little operation that I could not open my mouth, and as you have to feed the PEG down through the mouth to the stomach, and then bring it through the stomach wall, he could not do it. A few days later they decided to try again with me being given a general anaesthetic, but the anaesthetist refused to help unless I was put in a sterile operating theatre. She said that I had MRSA in my tracheotomy site and the operation was a dangerous one because if the bug got into my stomach it was goodbye to me. After a lot of organising, I was taken to the theatre to have a PEG put in. I was extremely nervous but I thought at least if everything went well it would mean I would also have my mouth open. Things went well, but I came back with my mouth still closed. I was relaxed, so it must have opened, and then when the anaesthetic wore off my mouth shut again. I was really disappointed!

My parents also asked at what stage they would consider removing my tracheotomy tube as this was what they were aiming for in HDU just before I was transferred. The other registrar said that my neck needed to be stronger first so that my head didn't flop forward and block my airway. Now just try putting your chin on your chest and see if you can still breathe. Exactly what he was qualified to be a doctor of, I am not certain.

I had now been in hospital for five months and Neo-Natal was anxious that Alexander went home. Simon kept putting it off saying he could not manage as he had gone back to work (which he had not as he had told me) but the doctor said that Alexander must go home or be transferred to another hospital. There was a meeting between Simon, his sister from London, my parents, a consultant, Ward Sister, Discharge nurse, me and my nurse and a vicar who was chairing the meeting. It was the most horrendous meeting ever.

Simon did not want Alexander home. I did not want him transferred to another hospital. The paediatrician was telling Simon that he did not bring Alexander to see me enough (Neo-Natal had allowed Simon to wheel Alexander over to see me in a pushchair as Alexander was healthy although he still needed oxygen). Simon said he could not afford the petrol to come all the way to Stoke more than twice a week. The argument got worse with me being so upset I had to be taken out of the room, but before I went, the doctor asked me what I wanted – hospital or home? I spelled out 'home'. As my nurse took me out of the room she said, "Dawn, he has got to go."

Then, for some reason, Simon brought my brother into the conversation saying that because Mark had offered to be Power of Attorney it meant that Mark wanted his house. My mother stepped in and an argument occurred between them with my mother excusing herself and walking out. The meeting broke up and Simon stormed out of the hospital. His sister said nothing. I think she was shocked at Simon's behaviour. He was like a child because he could not get his own way.

The paediatrician phoned my mother and asked whether we were really married because if not, they could do something about Alexander, but my mum said sadly, we were. The doctor said she'd had to go home and have a couple of Gin and Tonics, as she had never seen such bad behaviour as Simon's.

Alexander was discharged home in December and my parents offered their help to Simon. His sister from London said she would stay for a few days and between them, Simon would have plenty of help. My mother phoned Simon on Alexander's first night home and there was a commotion at the other end of the phone because a woman answered, Simon must have taken the phone off her and he tried to say it was on an answer machine when he was asked who it was.

I had another visit from the lovely lady from the Hayward Rehabilitation hospital. She came to assess me and I am glad to say I passed and I was transferred to the Hayward on December 15th. I was given the choice of transferring before or after Christmas; I went for as soon as possible. When I think about it now I don't know how I survived five months in a room alone with no means of calling for anyone. It makes me shudder!

Chapter 4

I was put in a ward with four other women and all of them with various illnesses. I made friends with two of them straight away and they kept an eye on me when my parents were not there. My parents had to cut the time down they spent with me as the visiting times at Haywood started at two p.m. and they stayed till nine p.m., (at the other hospital they came at twelve noon until nine p.m.).

Things went smoothly for a while. Simon would bring Alexander in the afternoons and stay a couple of hours. However, he soon started to ask my mother if she would take Alexander home with her and look after him for the night. It soon became a regular occurrence, with Alexander staying two or three nights with my parents. I was happy about the arrangement because it meant I had Alexander all day with me.

Christmas day Simon spent the whole day with me. The hospital provided a lunch for visitors so my parents stayed at home so that Simon, Alexander and I could spend our first Christmas together as a family; obviously I didn't realise at the time that it would also be our last. My parents came late afternoon and had tea with me. The hospital had put on a buffet and the day went well, I enjoyed it with my parents and Simon getting along fine, if only it could have stayed that way but it didn't! Things between them went from bad to worse!

Things at the hospital settled down into a routine and I received physiotherapy. Nowhere near as much as I thought, but some. The OT one day put me in an electric wheelchair and took me down the long corridor. It was so funny. I could not hold my head up and there was no head rest on the chair so a junior physiotherapist was assigned to holding my head. An OT was working the controls with my hand on them. Now the OT was quite a big girl and she had to run at the side of me but when we came to the door leading to the day room there was no way she was going to get through as well as my wheelchair. She shouted, "Look, Mum, no hands" then she let go. I went through the door with the physiotherapist behind and as I got inside the chair swung round because my hand slipped off the controls, the physiotherapist never let go, she just ran around with the chair. It was hilarious! I must say, they never tried it again, but what the OT did try was to help me feed Alexander. The physiotherapist sat me on a plinth with one physiotherapist sitting behind me and two others sitting either side of me. Alexander sat on a table in front of me. The OT held Alexander so with the physiotherapist holding my hand and arm we spoon-fed Alexander. He thought it was a game and he kept kicking his little legs and jigging about. If he liked his dinner he would eat OK but if not, the OTs and physiotherapists got covered. They only did it once without wearing aprons!

I did that a few times and really looked forward to feeding him but it stopped after Simon had another row with my mother. One day Simon's sister came and showed me a photo out of the blue. She said, "This is the woman who is going to look after your baby and Simon is going to bring her to meet you." I was shocked. Simon had mentioned about getting a childminder, but I said, 'Not while you are at home and you also have help from my parents,' but apparently he had gone ahead with it as Social Services were paying for her. I didn't want a stranger having my son. I wanted family to look after him I was so upset at knowing Simon had gone ahead and got a childminder that the physiotherapists had to cancel my test on my tracheotomy.

When my mother got home that night she phoned Simon and said how upset I was. She asked him not to take the woman to meet me until I had got used to the idea. At least let him tell me about this woman. Simon told my mother to mind her own business and slammed the phone down on her.

The next day a woman walked into the ward and introduced herself to me. Simon came in, trailing behind her. She then left the room. I disliked this woman instantly. I don't know what Simon had made up about my parents, but when they came, and the woman came back, she completely ignored them and Simon never attempted to introduce them.

Now that there was a childminder, my parents only had Alexander from Friday night after leaving me at about ten p.m. as it took them an hour to get home, till Sunday night ten p.m. but this soon stopped as I asked my mother to ask Simon if I could have Alexander in the day on Fridays so I could start feeding him again. Simon agreed, but said I could have Alexander at one p.m. on Friday till one p.m. on Monday, giving Simon a free weekend. Simon didn't visit me very much. I was heartbroken at his treatment of me.

Simon never kissed me when he came in. I think he thought he might catch my stroke. For all his faults, I still loved him very much and I would think never mind, I will sort him out when I am better. I had no idea that it was going to take me years, but Simon apparently had. I found out later that he had been on the Internet and read about the type of stroke I had had. Mine was a brain stem stroke which affected me from my throat down, leaving alone what they call the grey cells. When my parents had a meeting with my consultant he described me as having 'locked-in syndrome'. How I came to hate this phrase. It was a phrase Simon would throw back at me from time to time.

The more time I spent at Haywood the more *Carry on Doctor* started to look like reality TV. The mishaps at Haywood were generally quite amusing although some could have had serious consequences. Bearing in mind my condition of being unable to swallow and therefore strictly nil-by-mouth, it was probably not a good idea to pour mouthwash into my mouth and then ask me to spit it out (which I could not do), like one nurse did. Also at the time I was still having eye drops in an attempt to save my right eye. Unfortunately one day the drops were administered into my left eye. When questioned, the nurse stated that she did this because the right eye was closed! A million and one small mishaps continued to occur, such as a nurse giving me the buzzer in my hand one night and saying, "Press this if you need anyone." I must thank the nurses for their 'dippiness' which led to the funny story of the nurse who drove into town then forgot she had taken the car so caught the bus back home. Even so most of the nurses and care workers were very good to me, some would dye my hair for me and bring in DVDs, one night nurse would let me stay awake late to watch them.

The ward sister watched me one day when the physiotherapists were examining me and noticed I could move my head (thank goodness for me practising). She said I could sit out every day in a wheelchair for an hour or so. It was wonderful. I soon decided that I would try myself to sit out longer and set myself a target of seven hours, which it didn't take me long to reach.

I then had a wheelchair of my own ordered.

I had a lovely black nurse when I was at rehab. We became very friendly. She would come into my room when she was not busy and help me and my dad do the crossword. She got married while I was there and she came in on her wedding day to show me her dress. She looked beautiful. She now comes to my parents' home to see me and brings her little son Isaac with her.

I had one bad experience with a male bank nurse. It was in the early hours of the morning and I rang my bell for a bedpan, the bell that my parents had been given to attach to my pillow. By the time the nurse came it was too late and I needed to be changed. The female nurse left the room for a minute and I was left with the bank nurse. He was so disrespectful in his manner and language to me. He thought I was brain damaged. I was extremely upset. I thought about all the patients who WERE brain damaged and had to put up with his abuse and so the next morning I reported him. I don't know the full outcome of what happened but I do know he was banned from working on rehab again.

I never knew, but found out later that Simon and his sister had been in touch with the teachers association to see if they would fund the purchase of a special eye computer system that would enable me to communicate. It was from Canada. The Teachers Union Association gave enough money to fund the eye plus a laptop for me. When the eye came it was a heavy pair of glasses attached to a box. It was brilliant trying to work it. What you had to do was look at the corner, blink, then look at a letter and blink. I was finding it a bit hard to get the hang of it. One of the suppliers was coming to England for a holiday so he phoned my home and said he would call at the hospital to help me use it. He came and he was a great help. It was so kind of him but I found it too heavy for my nose to use it for any length of time.

My consultant said he knew of an association in Birmingham called ACT which could also help me. When ACT came, although they thought the eye was a brilliant idea, it cut off my only way of communicating with anyone if I was in distress as I could only see properly out of one eye. It had not been mentioned to the people in Canada. ACT asked if I had a computer. When I spelled out that I had a laptop, but that Simon had got it as he had taken it home, they said they would programme it for me to use with a gadget attached to my head rest that had a button on either side. All I had to do was to move my head from side to side and it would delete the word I didn't want until it came to the word I did, then it would print it for me.

The first thing I did was to write a letter to Simon. It took me nine days to write as it was not only a slow way of working but it was very tiring.

Here is my letter:

Simon, as you rarely can be bothered to let me talk; I have been compelled against best advice to write to you so once and for all you get my side of the story. No doubt you will decide that someone else has written this so although the evidence points otherwise you will believe what you want. Firstly I do not consider your actions as merely cruel, but barbaric, verging on sadistic. But why should you consider my pain when you have proved that your feelings for me must have been a sham as you have found me so easy to replace. As for giving

Alexander a 'normal' life, is playing happy families on holiday with him normal when his mother doesn't know where he is or how long he has gone for? For that matter as you are so rarely at Beech House I don't even know where he is living or sleeping. By the way who is looking after the cat, or should I add him to your list of abandonees? Your excuse of giving Alexander a normal life so you can enjoy yours is blatantly transparent, so you are really using him as a pawn. If you can recall, I had this stroke because I bore our beautiful son, but you think I should bear the burden alone. You cap this off by telling me you have the audacity to go to court, discuss the severity of my stroke, and offer me access rights of one day a month. Let me explain why it has got to court, to agree something amicably you must firstly let me talk and secondly answer my requests for contact, not just ignore it and expect me to agree to your terms. Or course any chance of an amicable agreement ceased on July 30th when you stopped my parents from bringing Alexander to see me, I know you have told a different tale, but we both know the truth of the matter. Although my family have stood by me and given support where you have not, it is still your aim to constantly denigrate and belittle them. It is always prudent to ensure your facts are correct before you slander people such as 'evil Uncle Mark', who wrote to Nottingham as my Power of Attorney to delay the procedure because I had received from you no information about what was being done. You originally told me it was a six-month programme; you have since decided it's a two-year programme, so the only person to blame for it being halted is actually you. As for the 'poison letter', do you really expect Mark to be civil after how you have treated his sister? Did you know I had received a similarly unpleasant letter from your sister disguised as a birthday card but she can be forgiven for only acting on your incorrect information. So when will you get it into your tiny mind that no one has ever been after custody, only now am I seeking access rights for reasons already stated. I have asked to see the document that purports to claim custody as nobody is aware of its existence, needless to say it has not been forthcoming. Why you have *persistently insisted that my family want custody is beyond me, especially as it was I who originally wanted Alexander to go home to live with his father. That is of course the same father who told neonatal that he couldn't have Alexander home because he had returned to work. By the way, you are right, it is medically impossible to cause a stroke but it is not medically impossible to cause additional stress for a person with already dangerously high blood pressure. I don't know if you remember your reaction to receiving a speeding fine on the Wednesday before my stroke, but I certainly do. Now you have actually started to regularly visit, well come for a short time once a week so I can briefly see Alexander, but you spend most of the time telling me how terrible it's been for you and bemoaning my family. I don't suppose you considered that while you had to go home alone there was a person who couldn't go home and because of circumstances will never see her beloved home again. Don't you think it is a little sick to have spent hours telling me how perfect I was for you while at the same time you had registered with dating agencies? You are well aware that I would have done anything for you but now you have ensured that the courts must agree my reasonable access requirements to our son. For your information I will get better and I will be back, that's fact and not conjectures. Dawn.*

I had Simon's letter posted to him and I also sent one to his father in Gloucester and his mother in Blackpool (they had divorced some years ago). I wanted them to know how their son was behaving towards me. Simon never had the decency to answer my letter or even mention it.

This was only the first of a letter writing frenzy, I wrote to my consultant because I disagreed with something he had said, the dietician because she had calculated my weight for my height and then had food administered appropriately, but I gained a lot of weight that I was not used to and I felt so uncomfortable. I also wrote numerous times to my friend in Scotland. On one occasion when I was letter writing a woman who was visiting her son came in to talk to my parents. 'Does she understand you? "She asked my parents. They replied that of course I could and that I was working on my computer, to which she added, 'But does she understand what she is writing?' I could not resist putting in my letter that there was a mad woman there who thought I was writing gobbledygook!

ACT had supplied me with a lot of equipment so I was put in a room of my own (my two friends had been discharged). I was looking forward to using my computer on a regular basis. ACT had also provided me with a bell for nights in case I needed a nurse. My parents would fix it to my pillow as mentioned previously, I used one of those travelling neck pillows as it kept my neck straight, otherwise it would lean to the left and I didn't have the strength to hold it straight myself for very long.

Chapter 5

One day Simon phoned the hospital and spoke to my mother asking her if she would pick Alexander up the next day and keep him for two weeks. The childminder had gone on holiday so he thought he would also have a holiday. He had already missed three weeks without coming to see me so this would mean it would be five weeks he had missed.

Simon's father phoned my parents' home to ask where Simon was as he had not been able to get in touch for some time. He never seemed to be in. My mother told him Simon was away. He asked about Alexander and my mother said they had him. My father-in-law was very cross; he said Simon was not taking responsibility for Alexander or me. He then told my mother that Simon had met another woman and it was the council that were paying for Alexander to be looked after. I wonder what tale he had told them because he most certainly was not at work. When I was told, I was devastated. I then understood why he was spending so little time with me.

I really should not have been surprised as once the wheelchair service went to my house to measure the width of our doorframes. Simon would not let them in as he said they were not knocking his door about, as it was a cottage. The warning bell should have rung then because it meant he was not having me back home and this was about seven months after my stroke Also a dead give-away was when I asked for my sandals, Simon brought in two pairs, one being mine and the other most definitely not mine as they were too big and clearly too frumpy to be my style.

After great thought I asked my brother to bring my cousin, who was a solicitor, to come to see me. I was going to finish with Simon.

I was going to divorce Simon on unreasonable behaviour. When he next came to see me I told him how much he had upset me, and all Simon said was, 'Well, I've done it before.' I was really taken aback to think that he didn't see that this time was different. He was also fond of telling people that he would never have divorced me, yet not once did he ever ask me not to divorce him. It is fortunate really as he certainly was not being a husband in sickness and in health!

I then started to have a number of blue dye tests done. This means that I had blue liquid put in my mouth to see if it would go down my throat and not on to my lungs. It was so that my tracheotomy could be downsized, ready for it to come out. They were also 'capping' me off to let me breathe through my mouth. The blue dye test would go well at one time but then they would decide to do another and that one would not go so well. They would do deep suction and there would be a little blue dye in my lungs but luckily I had a strong cough which prevented me from getting a chest infection.

I was also having a swallow test where the nurses would mix a little orange juice or blackcurrant with a thickening agent then stretch my mouth so they could put the mixture in my mouth at the back and see if I could swallow it by turning my head from side to side to keep the mixture at the back of my mouth because I could not move my tongue at all. It seemed to work although I had my off days where I did a lot of coughing and the test had to be stopped.

The capping off was working well. I was being capped off for a few hours in the day while my parents were there so they could keep an eye on my oxygen levels via a SAT's machine. It was a machine that checked the amount of oxygen in the blood. Sometimes it went down but would soon pick up again. (A bit stressful for all concerned). I was getting better and better at the capping off so they decided if I went 24 hours I could have my tracheotomy tube out. The first time I tried it, in the middle of the night, the nurse decided that I would not get any sleep with the machine because of the noise it made, so she switched it off. I could not sleep anyway for the disappointment and frustration I felt for not being able to tell her to leave it on. They tried again and I passed, but again I was disappointed as they then changed the goal posts and decided it would have to be forty-eight hours.

While they were trying to see if they could take my tracheotomy out my consultant referred me to maxillofacial to see if my jaw could be attended to so my mouth would open. The appointment went well but they decided it would be better for them to operate on my jaw with my tracheotomy tube still in. As my jaw needed to be opened, my tracheotomy was going to be left in until after my operation.

I had started divorce proceedings for Simon's unreasonable behaviour and the papers were served on him when he came back from holiday. Simon's mother was visiting me at the time I had decided on a divorce. She had come from Blackpool with Simon's other sister. This sister lived in Gloucester. When I told his mother she said, "I hope Simon lives to regret what he has done to you." Two months later Simon and my mother had another row. This time it was about Alexander's weekends with me. Simon had moved in with his partner, although he would not admit it. Simon decided he wanted to have Alexander at weekends now, as he wanted to spend more time with Alexander. Simon was not at work so my mother said he could have time in the week. Simon said 'no', it had to be weekends. It was obvious his partner worked in the week. He promised my mother she could have him on the Friday and then he got the childminder to ring up to say he had changed his mind and she could not have Alexander. Simon never let my mother bring Alexander again for about 6 weeks. Simon brought Alexander once a week for about an hour. On his first visit he asked me if I really wanted a divorce. I said 'yes'. I then not only had to go to court for my divorce, I had to go to court for contact with my son.

I had my operation, they took two small bones out one from each side of my jaw and cut a main muscle and my jaw was now open. I had to have a clamp put in for twenty-four hours. Having the clamp in was I think the worse part. My face was swollen the size of a full moon. My parents were ask if they wanted to stay overnight with me.

I am glad to say they did as I kept waking up but when I saw them there I would go back to sleep. The next day the clamp was taken out and in the afternoon Simon and Alexander came. My mother had mentioned to the childminder I was having an operation. It was very funny really because Simon had never brought me any flowers, even when I had Alexander. He only came to the hospital with flowers other people had sent for me, but this time he came with a bunch of flowers and a false tear in his eye, and immediately the nurse took the flowers away as flowers were not allowed in a surgical ward. I can imagine Simon's thoughts. It was wonderful to see Alexander.

After two days I went back to the rehab centre. I then had to start having my mouth stretched open with a clamp for five minutes twice a day. I was to have this done for five years. I was put on the waiting list to have my tracheotomy tube taken out as at the rehab they were not equipped to deal with an emergency if things went wrong, but I could not wait. One morning, while a nurse was changing the strap that holds the tracheotomy tube in place, I gave a big cough and my tracheotomy tube came out! I did not know because I never felt a thing. The nurse calmly pressed the emergency button and covered the hole in my neck. My consultant was informed and he said to send for an ambulance and send me into hospital for observation. The nurses kept their voices down so as not to upset me but when they told me what had happened I was so overjoyed I beamed from ear to ear (well the best I could!). It was my birthday – what a wonderful present.

In hospital I was told if I coped without the tracheotomy tube for forty-eight hours then that was it (no tracheotomy tube). My parents were informed and they came to me straight away. I was supposed to see Alexander as it was my birthday but we had no way of contacting Simon, as we didn't know where he lived. He didn't live at our matrimonial home, although he said he did.

In the afternoon, a message came from the rehab to say Simon was there with Alexander but he could not come to the hospital as he had been dropped off and the person was not coming back for him for an hour so I would not see Alexander. That was a blow but one and a half hours later Simon came in with Alexander. He stayed only fifteen minutes. At least I saw Alexander. He is so wonderful.

Out of the blue, on one of Simon's previous visits he asked me if I wanted Alexander christened. I could not understand this because we had talked about this subject when I was first pregnant. I wanted a christening but Simon did not (he is an atheist), so we agreed to let Alexander decide when he was older, so what I did was dictate three questions for Simon to answer. These are those:

1.   Why did an atheist want a christening?

2.   Who would we have for godparents as Simon would not want any of my family and I would not want strangers?

3.   How would we achieve a christening, as I would want to be there?

My mother gave him my questions when he visited me on my birthday. He never mentioned the christening again. I however started to think about it and my father asked the very nice Chaplin if he could come up with any ideas, which he did. He said he would christen Alexander at the hospital and that we did not need godparents as Simon and I could stand in. I waited for Simon to mention it again but he didn't and as he came when my parents weren't there and he never used my letter board anymore for me to ask him, it was not mentioned again until about nine months later.

I survived my 48 hours so I was sent back to the rehab hospital. I was so happy to be rid of my tracheotomy tube. I had had it in for fifteen months. My consultant said, "Dawn, you couldn't wait for the NHS could you? You had to do a DIY job."

Now that my tracheotomy tube was out it was pointed out to me that I would not have my 'Sats' checked so often, I could now wear nail polish. A nurse got me some lovely red polish, which she also applied for me on a number of occasions then she asked me what I would say to her if I could speak. I just could not resist – I said, "Bog off!" I should have said "thank you for all you have done for me" my joke backfired because she never did my nails again although she and a care worker used to dye my hair I was also able to go outside on a windy day, when my tracheotomy tube was in if any wind blew on me I would cough a lot. My parents took me out to see the green house were some of the patients were growing plants and tomatoes. They also took me a long walk round the rehab and hospital which was adjacent. With that and as my mouth was opening with help I was starting to feel like myself again; all I had to get sorted out now was my teeth and my eye.

Generally, when people have strokes their teeth go out of line but they normally go back again with a little time. Well mine didn't. The four bottom ones at the front lay flat; protruding out towards my lip, so this was another headache for the doctors. They could not understand why it had happened and what to do to right it. My teeth were to stay like they were for another two years, until a lovely African lady orthodontist took charge of my teeth.

Chapter 6

I settled down to not seeing Alexander as often as I used to as Simon had stopped the weekends so I concentrated on trying to get more physiotherapy which I never succeeded in doing. Really I was difficult for them because it took three physiotherapists at a time to handle me as I was like a rag doll. A lot of the time there was not that many free at the same time, although sometimes this had the effect of making me feel that I was too awkward to bother with.

Alexander had his first birthday at the rehabilitation and we had a party for him. His uncle, auntie, cousins and great-aunties came and we had a party in the physiotherapist's room. Alexander had a big red car for his birthday that could be pushed along while he sat in it although he had to have a cushion behind him, as he was so small. He was more interested in the big balloons that were attached to his car I had a lovely afternoon.

My divorce was going through. My brother and my cousin were dealing with it. Also, I had to apply to the courts for contact with my son. Simon's behaviour towards me got worse (if that was possible). He would come to the rehab and say such hurtful remarks to me, (which made my parents ask the nurses to try to hover around when he was there) he said things like I am going to tell the court the severity of your stroke and offer you one day a month with Alexander. He told me I would never get better and as I could not do anything for Alexander he could not understand why I wanted him. I was Alexander's mother and I loved him dearly. It broke my heart that when Alexander came to see me I had to be content to just sit there and watch him, without being able to hold him, cuddle him, kiss him.

Simon had already said to my parents, when he was in a temper, that I was a vegetable and Alexander, because he was deaf, very small and may have a sight problem, that he was a 'namby pamby' baby and that he would never make a 'Webster' as 'Websters' were born winners.

I hope Alexander never turns out to be a Webster, as Websters have no true feelings. I hate to generalise about a family but other than his mother and stepfather I have not heard from Simon's family for over four years.

My brother had my mail re-directed to his house as he was dealing with my finances and when my bank statement came through I found out that Simon had been on a dating agency to find other women. It was only five months after my stroke and our tiny son was still in hospital, yet all Simon could think about was women. What sort of a man had I been married to? My stroke had not affected my brain but I think it did something to Simon's.

As my divorce was still going through, my brother and cousin (solicitor) went to court to discuss my contact with Alexander. I was offered one day a week (Monday) from Simon, eleven a.m. till eight p.m., why I don't know, but I had to accept the one day and that is when CAFCASS got involved. A woman was assigned to my case, who later became Alexander's Legal Guardian and it was her job to check on how Alexander was being looked after. It did not seem to matter that Simon and his partner could not look after him and that they had to have a childminder because they were both at work. Simon had got a job working in the office at a police station (I won't tell you his opinion of the police before he got his job). I always wondered why he applied to them. (I found out a couple of years later). It seemed Simon could let anyone look after Alexander, but as I was an invalid and my parents were pensioners, my contact was to be limited with Alexander.

Simon was telling a great deal of lies about the rehabilitation and my family. When people sit listening to him they can be completely taken in by him. For example, Alexander's paediatrician wrote a letter to help Simon out when he went to court. She said that Alexander should not be allowed to come to the hospital to see me too often as it would be detrimental to him because some hospitals were dirty, and that he could pick up a germ that did not respond to antibiotics. Alexander would be a danger to the patients and to himself because he may pull their wires out and that he should not be around 'mental' people. She also said that she had read a book about my stroke and that it was going to take me years and years to recover. This doctor had never seen the 'hospital' as she called it - it is a rehabilitation centre, not a hospital. There are no patients 'wired up', they all go around in wheelchairs, except the MS people who have come in for respite. I had a room of my own so how would he come to any harm? And I objected to her giving a prognosis on me when she was not qualified to do so. I was extremely cross with the doctor and I asked my mother to go to see her and give her a piece of my mind which I dictated to my mother before she went. My mother also gave her a piece of her own mind as well! The doctor apologised when she heard the true story of how my parents and family had helped look after Alexander until the partner arrived. It seemed Simon was telling people that my family were trying to take Alexander away from him, which we have never done. He also said my parents only cared about me and never took any notice of Alexander. Like me, they adored Alexander.

The legal guardian came to the rehab to see me and she observed that Simon's story was totally untrue; Alexander was given the utmost care and attention.

Christmas was approaching and my mother spoke to the sister of the ward to see if I could go home for the festive season. I never thought they would agree but they said someone would check my parents' home to see how it could be arranged. Three people went to my parents' house. One was an OT; the other two were a discharge nurse and the lady that had first assessed me to be admitted to the rehab. It was decided that if my parents emptied their dining room, they would supply everything I needed to come home for Christmas. I became very excited at the thought of being allowed to go home, but I had to settle myself down and wait; my visitors helped me a great deal.

My friends from school had always kept in touch, they were all professional people who lived in various parts of the country and every so often would meet up to come and see me. I really enjoyed listening to tales of their busy lives. When my mother's two sisters came with one of my cousins it was like having a party, as they brought in a picnic. My aunts would bring in hot sausage rolls, cakes, mince pies and flasks of tea and coffee (although the rehabilitation centre provided facilities for making yourselves drinks). The conversation was so funny that I did not mind that I could not eat. I also had a visit from another auntie who was very entertaining, she is my father's sister and she is one of these sort of people who organizes everyone. It was early in the day when she arrived and immediately began to exercise my arms then she took me a walk and talked to everyone in the day room. By the time my parents arrived I was exhausted (I tire very easily) but it was lovely to see her. I also had many visits from patients' families. One man, whose wife came in for respite, would come and talk to my parents and me every night. He ran the London Marathon to raise money for the hospital and they bought me a lovely bouquet of flowers when I came home.

One young woman who I felt particularly sorry for was my age. Although she had had her illness for some years it went rampant when her second son was four months old. She could move and talk but she did not know any of her family. Her husband would rush in every night from work to sit with her and bring the children but alas when it was time for her to be discharged her family said they would not be able to cope with her at home. Her husband worked full time and her mother had to look after the children so she had to go in a home. I felt so sorry for her. It took me some time to stop thinking about her.

One lovely lady was the wife of a doctor and she said that her husband thought she was a witch so she said she would put the mockers on Simon (it still hasn't worked). I met some other nice people who visited their loved ones every day and I would get a little sad because Simon rarely visited.

Simon was causing another problem about Alexander. He kept telling me that Alexander needed a cochlea implant and that the hospital was only waiting for a date to operate on him. I was concerned, as I had not been informed about any of Alexander's hospital appointments or any outcomes. I asked my brother to write to the consultant to put a hold on things until I had some information on what a cochlea implant was. The hospital stopped everything and sent me a lot of literature on implants. From their letters, it seemed that Alexander was only going into hospital for a test, not an operation. They had to determine whether he was suitable or not. It took a year for everything to be sorted out. Simon was going mad at my brother's intervention. He threatened to have him prosecuted for child cruelty (what an idiot). My family and I had always insisted that Alexander could hear, especially men with deep voices, like his granddad. Alexander always acknowledged when his granddad spoke. Luckily, one day when a gentleman from the Hearing Impaired Centre came to see me and Alexander, he was amazed that when my father stood behind Alexander and told Alexander to do something, Alexander did it, which meant that he had not seen his lips move or guessed what he was being asked to do. The gentleman said that they would have to be careful when the test was done because Alexander could hear and a cochlea implant would destroy any hearing he had.

I will never understand why Simon was pushing so hard for Alexander to have an implant. Why make Alexander go through his life with a cochlea implant when a hearing aid will help him hear? (A cochlea implant is perfect for children with no hearing). Alexander had the test done (which they did while he was sedated) and I am happy to say he did not fit the criteria for an implant, although Simon still tried to upset me. He phoned the rehab and after the test was completed he left a message to say that Alexander did need one and they were waiting for a date to operate. Luckily, my brother had been in touch with the hospital and gave me the true story. Why did Simon try to hurt me any way he could?

My parents stripped the dining room, sold some of their furniture and spread the rest around the house. My first day home was Dec the thirteenth, just for a trial run. It was a Monday, the day I had Alexander, but Simon again decided that he didn't want me to have Alexander (Simon must have somehow found out I was coming home), although it was a court order. The childminder phoned to say I could have Alexander for two hours instead of the day I had been given and that was only if she stayed with him. I had to agree because I wanted to see Alexander in my home, playing, sitting in his high chair, rolling around on the carpet. Although it was only two hours, it was wonderful. I felt so relaxed being home and Alexander loved it. When it was time to go back to the rehab, although they were good to me, I dreaded going back.

When I returned to the rehab centre I started to go to the day room on occasions because the activity manager ran some quiz games and I love quizzes, I won quite a few times, he also had Bingo games and would try to get me to play but if there is one game I do not like it is Bingo when I first arrived at the rehab The manager who was a pleasant man came to me and asked if there was anything he could do for me so I suggested writing a diary which he did right up until the time I had my computer. The manager was also a motorbike enthusiast and as I was also keen on them he would talk about his, he had three bikes and he would come to work on different ones so my parents would take me outside to see them.

I next went home on Christmas Eve and I was to have Alexander on Christmas Day. Simon wanted Alexander on the Christmas afternoon so he said that I could have Alexander Christmas Eve, all day, but he would not confirm it with his solicitor or with anyone else except my mother. Simon must have thought that as in the past my mother would go along with what he wanted just to keep the peace. She had often joked him out of a bad temper. When we were on holiday and Simon was in a temper my mother would say he is hungry so get him a pasty (this seemed to help calm him down and from then on he was nicknamed nasty pasty). Simon had lived with my parents for two years before we bought our first house so Simon must have believed that he could get round my mother, but he was grossly mistaken. First and foremost I was her daughter and his treatment of me was appalling.

When she took Alexander back on Monday the twentieth well I think the atmosphere was explosive when he told my mother that I had not been told two p.m. and that he had said twelve noon.

This is the conversation:

Mum: "My daughter does not tell lies."

Simon: "No, but she has got it wrong, I never said two p.m. I told my solicitor twelve noon."

Mum: "No you didn't, you would not give her an answer and she has parted company from you, you no longer have a solicitor. You are the biggest liar that ever walked this earth. You are spiteful and vindictive."

Simon: "You will never have Alexander again. Dawn will only see him through a third party. Get out of my house."

Mum: "It is not your house. It is half my daughter's."

Simon then went over to my mother with his hand raised. My mother stood in front of him and said, "Just you try it, Simon." He then dropped his arm and my mother realised he had been going for the door.

Simon: "Get out, or I will call the police. You will never set foot in this house again."

Mum: "That's OK; I will pick Alexander up in the drive."

Simon then turned and went to the hall where the phone was. He bent down to dial and my mother leaned over his shoulder and said, "When the police come, I will tell them that you have fraudulently re-mortgaged this house," then she turned and went out. She sat outside the house with my father and waited, because as she said, if the police *did* arrive, she was not having him tell a pack of lies. Simon had Alexander in his arms all the time the row was going on. Alexander woke up once when Simon shouted at my mother, rather than being upset as Simon later claimed.

I know Simon would not be able to cope with a face-to-face argument. He liked to write letters or phone people to complain.

Simon came out of the house and went to go to his car. He did not have Alexander with him but when he saw my parents were still sitting in their car he ran back into the house.

My solicitor received a letter two days later. In it Simon said my mother was deranged, that *she* had gone to hit *him* that she had upset Alexander with her shouting and he wanted a letter of apology!

On Christmas Eve the childminder phoned my mother and said she would bring Alexander round if my mother gave her a letter of apology. My mother asked me what to do as she had not done what he accused her of. She felt it was wrong to write the letter, but for my sake she would. I told her not to let Simon blackmail us so she told the childminder 'no'. The childminder said to just give her a blank piece of paper, as she knew my mother would not have done what he said but she stipulated that the envelope had got to have Simon's name on it. The childminder was upset when my mother again said 'no' because she felt Simon would have put the envelope to some use against her. The irony was that a number of years earlier my mother had shielded Simon from a physical attack; he knew full well that she would not have gone to hit him.

Simon's anger was getting out of control. I did not have Alexander over Christmas and it was the seventeenth of January before I was able to give Alexander his Christmas presents. Even so, I saw Alexander on New Years Day when Simon brought him to see me and said it was my mother's fault I did not have Alexander at Christmas. I saw him again on Monday the tenth of January for an hour. I had a shock when the childminder came walking in with Alexander in her arms. It was my day to have Alexander, and I know my parents every Monday since my mother's row went and sat outside my home, waiting for Alexander to be handed over. In actual fact, when the neighbours told Simon that they had been waiting outside, Simon wrote to my solicitor to say that they were spying on his house.

I did not want the childminder there because I did not like her. I spelt out to the nurses that I wanted her to leave Alexander with the nurses and me. The childminder refused to leave, saying Alexander was in her care. Did she not understand that I am Alexander's mother, whether I can move or not? The despair I felt inside, that I could do nothing, but watch her holding my son. When the nurses hold him, or my family and friends hold him I have this feeling of pride because they are holding him for me, but the childminder I felt wanted to take over him. I had already told Simon I didn't want to see her or him again and I asked the rehab hospital to ban him.

I wrote this letter to Simon and I also wrote the childminder a letter, although I did not like the childminder out of principle, I felt she was good for Alexander and he thrived with her;

Simon, as you have treated this divorce as a green light to happily make a guilt-free life for yourself instead of the wakeup call it should have been, I no longer want you to visit. Your behaviour has been as if I no longer exist and you are now only coming to see me out of some misplaced sense of duty, as you don't even bother to enquire how I am doing. Perhaps if you did you would be aware that I no longer have locked-in syndrome. If you recall the very last scene of Farscape, I'm sorry to say that is exactly what it feels like you have done to me. I suppose it must make you feel like a real big man to have given up on your wife and completely destroyed her at the time she needs you the most. You are fond of saying that Alexander will never beat the champion, that's champion coward as far as I can tell, the man who let his wife have his child then abandoned her as circumstance made her of no use to him. I need not concern myself that reading this truth might upset you; the only real emotion that you must be capable of is anger. You have shown by your lack of reaction to my previous letter that you don't have the guts to apologize, or worse that in some warped way you believe that your actions are wholly justified. If this sounds like an outpouring of angry resentment, that's because it is. How do you expect me to feel when I loved you enough to have your child, with disastrous consequences, but you didn't love me enough to stand by me? I suppose I can only blame myself for not realising you were so weak. There was no point in displaying my anger when you visited me, as explaining why, assuming you noticed, would have been impossible. Another good reason for you not to come again is to spare me sight of your revolting new collection of shirts. I can only assume they look cheap and nasty because they are. That probably won't bother you as I'm sure my opinion is no longer valid. An arrangement which would suit your busy schedule would be to allow my parents to bring Alexander up then either you or Sue could collect him a couple of hours later. That way you wouldn't have to come in and your pretence that I no longer exist would be complete. No doubt this letter will make you arm yourself with more lies and please don't think I was naïve enough to have only sent you a copy of that previous letter. I am sure many more people know my side by now. So goodbye, go live your new life. Dawn

Chapter 7

I was having regular physiotherapy at this time as I had a lovely physiotherapist who seemed to want to see how much of me moved. Whatever I moved, it was only slight, but it meant that the messages were getting down from my brain. My stroke was something to do with the white cells at the base of my skull which control all movement and muscles and it would take years for them to repair.

One day the physiotherapist said to my parents that if they went down the road to ASDA and brought me a swimming costume, she would take me to the hydro pool. It was absolutely marvellous and although my body movements were not any easier it was so lovely being in the water. While having physiotherapy in the water I would imagine I was in the sea and if I concentrated enough I might be able to go swoosh and lift my arms right up into the air like a wave, but no matter how hard I tried I could only make tiny ripples. Some movements like moving my arms away from my body; I just do not know how to do. With my hands I know I have four fingers and a thumb but can only move two fingers and my thumb very slightly; I can feel my little finger but it seems to be taunting me and saying, "no matter how much you try, I am not moving." I went in the hydro pool twice more but then my physiotherapist left to live in Canada because she had promised her boyfriend that she would join him out there where he was studying. I then had a pleasant male physiotherapist who gave me regular physiotherapy but he was moved to the outpatients department. So I had to again struggle on.

I have all my senses, I can taste, smell, feel hot and cold and I know my voice box is intact because I had a test, but it is difficult to get enough air in my lungs to force out words. I can manage some when I am lying down, as I can fill my lungs easier.

I was having my mouth stretched twice a day. In the morning the nurses did it so they could clean my teeth and them every evening by my mother. My parents came every day and stayed from lunch time until about eight-thirty – nine p.m., except on a Monday, when they had to leave at seven p.m. to get Alexander back to his father by eight p.m. That was the one day I had been given. Simon was originally going to offer me one day a month to see my son.

My consultant was always good to me. He helped me not only with my health by giving me a number of Botox injections to help my muscles and saliva but also with my contact case. He wrote a number of letters to my solicitor to be used in court. He also wrote a letter for me to give to Simon, as Simon would bring 'locked-in syndrome' in his conversation with people all the time. My consultant wrote that I now did not fit the criteria. There were two registrars, one female and one male and they were also very friendly to me. The woman registrar liked to hold Alexander.

My parents were being helped a great deal with their meals by my aunty preparing for them and my sister-in-law's mother used to phone my parents as they were going home to say she had a meal ready for them and when they called, Val would have a lovely meal ready for them on a tray to take home. Another aunty made them beautiful sponge cakes and flans

I was to have a meeting to see about regular visits home, and I am pleased to say they were going to allow me to go home Sunday to Wednesday. I was given a bed with a ripple mattress, a nebuliser and suction machine because I coughed a lot and as I was not able to swallow, it needed to be used to suck the excess saliva out of my mouth.

The ambulance men were marvellous. They would manoeuvre my stretcher down the hall and then with twists and turns they got me through the dining room door. My father would follow the ambulance after he had dismantled my chair and put it in his car. My mother travelled with me.

I was then assessed later for going home permanently. I was going to take over my father's garage. Half would be my bedroom, the other half the wet room. It was only a single garage so it was quite small but I would have lived in a shoebox if it meant that I could go home.

It was at this time that I was to receive another shock by what Simon and his partner had done to me. My brother received a redirected letter from our home insurance company to say our policy had lapsed, which made me worry as all my jewellery plus personal belongings were in the house. Simon was away on holiday so because he had taken my parents' key; my father went to the estate agent to ask for my keys. My home had been up for sale for about a year. After my father told them the situation, they gave him the keys. My parents went into the house and my mother found a card that congratulated Alexander on his baptism. It was a great shock to them. My parents did not tell me, as they wanted to be certain what the card meant. My mother phoned the legal guardian to tell her and to ask her if she would find out if Simon and his partner had baptised my son behind my back. When the legal guardian asked Simon, he categorically denied having Alexander baptised, so my father went round to our church. We are Church of England but the vicar said no one had been baptised by the name of Webster. When my mother thought about it she said baptism is Catholic so my father went to the Catholic Church and the priest there remembered the baptism because Simon and his partner led him to believe I was in a coma. The priest was quite upset that he had been misled. He gave my father a copy of the baptism certificate. On it were the names of Simon's sister from London, his half-sister and his partner's son and the address of her house, which they had both denied he lived at.

I was devastated when I heard. It was something I had wanted to have done but Simon had said, "No, let's leave Alexander to decide when he grows up."

It was one of the subjects we discussed before Alexander was born. Simon was not a believer in religion. The hurt I felt was that Simon could have Alexander baptised for his partner of five months and yet he would not have a christening for me. He must have been desperate to please her. I know Simon; it was to his advantage to keep in with her as she was the roof over his head. The priest came to see me at my parents' home. He was extremely sorry but Simon and his partner had been so convincing. The priest said he overlooked the fact that they were living in sin but they made the priest believe Simon had no one else to help him. There was nothing I could do about it until my aunty spoke to her local vicar and she said that I could have Alexander blessed and she would add my brother and his wife to be Alexander's godparents. I was thrilled and I started to plan my son's christening (although it would not be a christening; it would be a blessing).

The first chance I got, I went on the Internet and bought Alexander a lovely cream suit, with matching shirt and tie. He looked wonderful in it. The blessing was also wonderful. The vicar did everything the same as a christening except for the water over Alexander's head. The woman vicar had left the church by the time the blessing was organised but I had a most wonderful male vicar step in to do the blessing. He came to see me first to explain the service and I must say he made the service perfect. My family and friends then went to my auntie's, who lives just down the road from the church, for refreshments. Alexander, I think, loved the limelight.

I started to progress with my fight for contact with Alexander although, because of Simon's dislike for my cousin and brother, they had to stand down from my case and I had to appoint another solicitor at much more cost, so much so I had to apply then for legal aid. Everyone concerned said it was to ease the 'aggro'.

I came home permanently in June 2005. I had been in hospital and rehab for two years. The garage, although promised, was not even started on, so I stayed in the dining room, but I did not mind. I was home!

For the next eight months I had to have bed baths (our bathroom was upstairs) and my parents washed my hair in the garden on sunny days and in the sink on wet ones. The kitchen used to be flooded! I have such long hair and due to my medication my hair became greasy so quickly.

When I left hospital they wanted to fit a catheter in me to make things easier when I was at home but I was defiantly against the idea. I felt I would never get control of my toileting if this happened. In rehab, the nurses were not always free when I would say I needed the pan and it was too late by the time they were. I so wanted to be able to control my toilet habits. I knew my parents would help me and I am happy to say it worked and now I can even go out for the day and use the public disabled toilets with the help of my parents.

When I was home permanently I started to go to a day centre for a day where I would watch the other patients play games or they would have a quiz. Obviously, I could not join in, so I simply sat and watched. Then the physiotherapist would come and take me for physiotherapy and then the OT would also come and take me for some hand exercises, but alas it was short-lived. After six weeks a meeting was held and I was to be discharged as the day centre only allowed six weeks. My parents were appalled as they said, 'What will happen to her recovery, no matter how slow, if there was no help at all?' All they were told was to keep moving my arms and legs, as any movement would help. The physiotherapists said they would review me in three months' time but the OT just cut me off so my recovery was basically down to my family. The physiotherapist did explain that weekly physiotherapy would not show recovery. Recovery would only show in months.

One thing the physiotherapist did suggest was that if I could stand every day then that would help with strengthening my legs and my internal organs. To do this, I would need to buy a standing chair; this is an electric wheelchair which would raise me up into a standing position with me strapped into it. The problem was that it cost £20,000 so with the help of my brother and sister-in-law who found out about charities that may help, the fund-raising started. If things had gone to plan when I was divorced, and I had got the allowance the judge had given me (which was three quarters of the sale price of our house) I could have bought the wheelchair myself, but because Simon never lived in our home, and would not allow my family near it, the house was a mess and in the end it had to be auctioned off so instead of about £60,000 I got £12,000. This is something I will never understand, as Simon loves money. Was it to spite me or did he have to let it go before it was re-possessed?

Chapter 8

I managed to get help from three charities plus other sources, so I ordered a standing wheelchair. As I couldn't move my hand or arms, I had to have a control fitted so that I could use my chin. The first time I used it I went out in the garden and I followed Alexander all around but found it was extremely tiring to use. I started standing in it for fifteen minutes and slowly built it up to one hour. It was a bit scary at first but I was securely strapped in with a belt around my chest and another blocking my knees. For long stands I have an adjustable table set in front of me supporting an easel on which I have a book so I can read while standing, my arms supported on two pillows that are laid across the end of the table.

Many others helped me raise the funds for my chair, My PA's mother-in-law who was a care worker at Stafford hospital collected a hundred pounds from her colleagues to go towards my chair. Many other people had helped along the way. My cousin was the manager of ASDA in Tipton and the women on his Deli counter raised money for Alexander and bought him a Maclaren pushchair, a basket of toiletries and a set of towels. My uncle also helped out.

I had a party to celebrate being home a year and I found my chair was excellent because I could raise it up while I was still in a sitting position and be on eye level with my friends while they were talking to me.

My family started to do my physiotherapy themselves and with the aid of my standing chair I thought maybe I will get somewhere with my recovery. I know nowadays that everything is controlled by money and it seems that patients are the last to be consulted. If only someone thought about people instead of how much money they can save if they stop certain, long-term people's physiotherapy. I felt lost and frustrated when mine was stopped. Although my family helped me, I still felt unless I got professional help and wondered what would happen to me.

My professional physiotherapy was to be every three months but then my mother asked my doctor if he could do something and so it went down to two months, then one month and then I went on holiday in 2008 and because my family had to stand me for toileting, dressing me, getting me in and out of bed, which altogether was about ten times a day, (because although I had hired a manual hoist, my parents forgot to take my sling and I had also hired a shower chair instead of a toilet chair), when I went back to the physiotherapists they said I was a thousand times better. So it shows that physiotherapy is the treatment all patients need, long-term or short-term. I am happy to say I have physiotherapy once a fortnight now and my physiotherapists are very good to me.

Chapter 9

Now that I was out of rehab my contact for Alexander was well underway. My brother and my cousin had been to court twice but on the first occasion Simon didn't turn up. He was now acting for himself. As I previously said, he and his solicitor had parted company. I don't know who was helping him but since he went to work in an office at a police station, he seemed to think he had the backing of the police force. He was always threatening my family with the police. It started with my cousin because he had disclosed to Simon's then solicitor that Simon had been fraudulent and he had also written to Simon's sister in London. Simon went mad. He threatened my cousin with the Law Society. He also said that the police were investigating him (all of which was make-believe). Simon then went on to my brother. He sent the police to my brother's home to have him arrested for opening a letter belonging to him. This letter was mistakenly re-directed to my brother's house by Royal Mail and as my brother was receiving all my mail by re-direction, he took it to be mine. Once he realised it was Simon's, he sent it to my solicitor for him to deal with. I have never wanted to get Simon into any trouble, or his sister, but when he did this to my brother I told Mark to tell the police about the fraud. The allegations against my brother were dropped but Simon's fraudulent dealings were reported to the serious crime squad.

Simon's partner had also started to threaten my parents with the police.

On one occasion, my father took Alexander back to Simon after my contact day. He was met by a woman standing on the pavement at the bottom of our drive. She asked for Alexander. My father said "no" as he did not know her and she said she would fetch the police if he did not pass him over. My father still said "no" and asked where Simon was. The woman said, "In the house, but he does not want to see you." My father would not hand Alexander over until they went into the house. Simon had been served with a writ that night and he was extremely cross. It was to make him disclose his finances.

On another occasion, Simon's partner sent the police to my parents' house alleging harassment. All that had happened was that Simon's partner had put a letter through my parents' door asking my mother to take Alexander to hospital for an ear appointment, but asked if she would put the answer through to our old address. Why? As my mother knew he lived with his partner at her home (which was about two minutes by car across the road from our house). My mother put her answer through Simon's partner's door. We then got another letter saying he did not like the tone of my mother's letter, so my mother could not take Alexander to his appointment, but she or I could meet the childminder at the hospital and bring Alexander back with us. (It was my contact day). My mother answered this letter by saying she would meet the childminder but as I was paralysed and in a wheelchair, I would not be able to meet the childminder. She said, "I know it is such a trivial matter to you, you have obviously forgotten." The next thing we knew was a policeman at the door. He came into our house saying he could take my mother to the police station for a couple of hours as they take harassment extremely seriously. My mother said she could prove Simon lived with his partner, but the policeman did not want to see any proof. My mother then told him about the detective sergeant from the Special Crime Squad that had visited me for a chat about the fraud, to hear my side of the story and to tell me they were going to arrest Simon. The policeman said that he knew the detective sergeant as he had worked with him, so he would be getting in touch with him to let him know the situation between the two families.

Simon was arrested the following week. He was released on police bail. We never heard any more about the fraud until we had a meeting with the legal guardian about four or five months later and she said the case had been dropped. My mother phoned the DS and he said we should have had a letter from the Crown Prosecution Service and he would check what had happened. Another month went by before we had the letter and it said that the mortgage company (Halifax) wouldn't produce any evidence and that the court felt it was "not in the public interest for the police to pursue it." Not only did Simon get away with fraud, he stayed working at the police station and he was also allowed to join the police force as a 'special' constable. Unbelievable!

Months later, while we were out shopping, we saw Simon's partner. She was in a police uniform and everything began to fall into place I then realised where Simon had been getting all his information. If I had known she was a policewoman when she told us about Simon not living with her and when she sent the police to my parents' home, I would have reported her for using her position in the police to intimidate my parents.

There were a few other times that Simon had claimed money falsely. He had written to my school and asked them not to reduce my maternity salary as, if they did, he may have to sell our home and it would be a shame for me when I wanted to come home. And yet, when I was to have a wheelchair made for me and the wheelchair service went to my home to measure the door opening, Simon would not let them in as he said, "This is a cottage and you are not knocking it about." I think that showed that he never intended me to go back to him.

Simon also wrote to my union about getting some extra money to live on. He had already had a few thousand pounds for my eye computer from Canada and he still wanted more. The union sent him two cheques of seven hundred and fifty pounds each. I never saw any of this money or even knew about it. It was only when the bank statement and letters came to my brother's house that it was discovered.

Simon told everyone that he re-mortgaged so that I would not be blacklisted. He said our loans that we had had were because I loved clothes and shoes and going on holiday. Yes I loved clothes and shoes but if I remember correctly we both loved holidays. Our first big loan was for Simon to buy a Toyota MR2 and pay off his gold card and the second of fourteen thousand pounds was to buy me a three thousand pound second-hand car, which Simon did up and sold later and brought himself a motorbike with all the extra money. Simon had twenty thousand pounds out of the re-mortgage. He never even paid my credit card off.

Now that I was home permanently, the court case was developing with me getting two days a week with Alexander, but because of Simon's arrest, he refused to let me see Alexander. I was to go ten weeks without seeing him. Simon would have nothing to do with my family so it was suggested that a third party be appointed. That way, Simon would not have to meet any of them. As no one seemed to be doing anything about my not seeing Alexander and it was seven weeks since I had seen him, my sister-in-law's mother offered to help. She lives about five minutes away. My mother rang the legal guardian with the suggestion and it was agreed by her. After she had made two visits to my sister-in-law's mother and father to make the arrangements that it could go ahead, my parents went to court and although Simon shouted at my father and said he would not take or collect Alexander from my sister-in-law's parents' home and neither would his partner, the judge said, "Yes you will, Mr Webster." He also said that he did not mind *me* seeing Alexander, but he did not want my parents to see him and the judge said, "That's a bit difficult as she lives with them." He also said that when he phoned my home, my mother was not to answer the phone. Obviously he had a special ring.

My contact was then resumed.

I thought at first that Alexander would not remember me or my parents but as soon as his granddad went to pick him up Alexander was so excited to be seeing us all again.

When Simon abandoned me I felt lost. I was totally destroyed. I could not believe that in such a short time he could walk away. I thought I must have grown another head or something. I lost all my confidence to meet certain friends or colleagues from work. That was until my friend in Scotland came to visit me. He had been emailing me every day. I had put him off for eighteen months after I came out of rehabilitation, but then he bought tickets for the NEC to see *War of the Worlds* and he said he would love to take my brother and me with him to see it. I reluctantly said yes, but it was marvellous when he came. He sat by me and talked and talked. He said I was still Dawn and he gave me my confidence back. Just a few weeks later I visited my colleagues at school, taking Alexander with me I also started to go to the cinema with my brother and family.

Many more court cases were to come and I was able to go as I had been given an adapted car through the Mobility Scheme. I settled down to my fight for more contact with Alexander.

I seemed to be forever writing letters and having meetings. The meetings were to be held at my home but Simon must have said something, which would have been totally untrue, so when the first meeting was held it was all cloak and dagger stuff. My parents were banished to the kitchen and Alexander's solicitor fetched Simon from his house (five minutes' walk from mine) and the legal guardian had to answer the door. My parents were not allowed to show their faces. I had an advocate sit with me. The advocate was an excellent young man that used to visit me in hospital and give me advice. At these meetings Simon could say anything he liked, true or untrue and I could only spell out to my advocate a few words. I could not voice my opinion, as this would have taken too long. At one of the meetings, Simon dropped a bomb on me: he asked for parental responsibility for his partner. I crumbled inside. I knew what everyone had been hinting at was true and he wanted me out of Alexander's life. All the love I had for Simon evaporated. All I felt was pity for him because he had become so bitter and cruel and easily manipulated. I will never forgive him. I had lost everything I loved;

my job, my home, my husband, my way of life and now Simon and his partner wanted to take my son away from me. This woman has two adult sons of her own. What sort of a person is she? She said she needed PR for getting information at his hospital appointments but the childminder had no trouble in getting the information for Simon.

Chapter 10

I decided I had to do something to stop going mad so I enrolled on an Open University Degree. I had always been interested in history, so I took an Honours degree in Ancient History, which I found hard work but extremely rewarding.

In between court battles, I was trying hard to improve my body. I was given ten hours for a personal assistant from the Independent Living Fund and my PA was a wonderful person. We became good friends. She would take me shopping and I could spot a bargain before she could. She said she did not know how I did it considering I only had one eye. My excellent ophthalmologist had treated my eye every time I had an eye infection. He would come to see me every day and sometimes if he had been busy it would be ten p.m. I am afraid all of the ophthalmologist's hard work in trying to save my eye came to nothing. I lost my vision. Then my eyeball sank and I had a shell put over my eye for cosmetic purposes. My PA worked hard on my physiotherapist every time she came. She was with me for eighteen months, and then she got a job in a hospital as a physiotherapy assistant, full time.

I was also having regular visits from a speech and language therapist. When I first came out of hospital I was visited from time to time by someone from the speech and language therapy centre, but it was infrequent until a friendly therapist visited me and she helped me a great deal. So much so, she helped me to start taking food. I started with yoghurts and progressed to anything I liked, as long as it went through a blender. I only ate a small amount. She also showed my mother how to put ice on my face to help the right side of my face to have some movement in it, and to help my lips to move as well as putting ice inside of my mouth which helped me to swallow. The main thing was that it helped my tongue to move and I can now almost put my tongue out at Alexander!

My speech and language therapist has been training to be a vicar and as she has qualified she has now moved on, but before she went she got an OT to take some interest in my hands and I was visited a few times by an OT who made me some hand splints – the ones I had come out of hospital with had become uncomfortable. I also visited the hospital at the OT's request to have my splints checked but alas, I have not heard from her now for months, so I am hoping someone else will take her place, as I really need someone to help with my hands. My family stretch them and get me to move my thumb, which although I first moved a fraction while in rehabilitation, I can still only move about three fractions now, two years later. Although they said my recovery would be slow, I think that it is an understatement.

I was having meetings with Simon at my home and my parents were still being banished out of Simon's sight. My parents, although they had been taken on board as the solicitor called it after the first court appearance and Simon's episode of shouting at my father, they were taken off my case again. It seemed that whoever Simon doesn't like, they have to be removed. Simon didn't have a solicitor – he was acting for himself. I think acting for yourself is a good idea because Simon seemed to be getting away with everything. He broke a lot of court orders, he constantly wrote untruths and my parents had to get letters from various people to prove he was telling untruths constantly.

Also, his partner was also making things up. At some time I had an appointment with a school I was hoping Alexander would attend, but when I arrived with my parents, Simon's partner was in the classroom with Alexander. I went into the headmaster's office and he told me they were there. I immediately looked at my mother and she told the headmaster that if Alexander saw we were there he would want to come home with us, as he has done on a number of occasions, especially if he sees his granddad. The headmaster told Simon's partner the situation, but a letter was sent by Simon, to the solicitor, later that week, to say I had refused to see my son because he was with Simon's partner and that I hate her. The headmaster sent a letter to my solicitor to prove otherwise.

Alexander had also been prescribed high-energy milk when he was discharged from hospital. Alexander's doctor would give my parents a prescription from time to time, as Simon has stopped sending any milk when my father fetched Alexander on my contact day. Simon found out from the chemist that we were giving Alexander this milk and he went crazy, writing to the solicitor to say Alexander had had the milk stopped some twelve months previously and that it was dangerous for him to still be having it. Yet, on checking with the chemist, we found that Simon had put a prescription in himself for the milk in the September, although he had not collected it. When we put ours in, at the beginning of November, we had to get a letter from the doctor to prove that the milk was not dangerous and should only be stopped after Alexander had seen a dietician.

My case with Simon was becoming so silly. I wrote to him to ask him to share Alexander with me, and just get on with living his life, the life that he has now. Simon was obsessed with causing trouble for my family, especially for my father as he was the one who collected and returned Alexander. My mother had never spoken to Simon since the row over my contact at Christmas 2004, four years ago. The childminder had given up her position after twenty months. Simon told my father that she left because she did not like the 'aggro' when she handed Alexander over to him. My father could not understand this as nothing had ever happened. Simon must have thought this was funny because he told the childminder what he had said to my father. While my father was out shopping, the childminder came up to him and said that Simon had no right to say what he had said, because it had nothing to do with my father why she left. She did not say the reason she *had* left and my father did not ask, but we had our own ideas.

Alexander had another childminder who did not stay long and then he was sent to a nursery and although he settled in there, I think he was a little isolated from some of the children. Because of Alexander's deafness, he could not talk, he could only babble and it was hard for other children to understand him. Even at the nursery, Simon could not leave my father alone. Alexander and his granddad had such a good relationship; in fact the nursery said Alexander was 'Granddad mad'. There was a game Alexander and Granddad played. My dad would playfully put his fist up to Alexander and say, "Come here, and I will punch your nose." Alexander would lovingly run to his granddad and Granddad would put his fist on Alexander's nose. Alexander would laugh with delight. When Alexander was at nursery he tried to say it to the nursery nurse but she could not understand him so she asked Simon. He did not know what Alexander was trying to say so he asked my dad. My Dad said, "I will show you," and he played the game with Alexander. Two days later I received a letter from Simon to say Alexander had been threatening to punch the noses of all the other children. My father went to the nursery to apologise and explain about the game he played with Alexander. The nursery said they knew nothing at all about it. They said he had laughingly said it once to his favourite nursery nurse. I immediately wrote to Simon to tell him and he just wrote back to say, "Well it is a silly game to teach a child." I think someone should teach Simon to grow up.

More meetings were held at my home with my parents banished to the kitchen and I weathered them all with my excellent advocate until I thought 'enough is enough' and I suggested we had meetings on neutral ground, so it was suggested we meet at Alexander's Solicitors' office in Stafford. Meetings were arranged but Simon would always make some excuse and not turn up. We never again had a joint meeting. The legal guardian and Alexander's solicitor would meet me at my home and Simon and his partner at their home. Then disaster struck: My parents had an accident with Alexander while making some *Thomas the Tank Engine* cakes. Alexander burnt his bottom on the right, just on the side of his spine. We did not know exactly how he did it. All I saw was him fall backwards against the oven door. My mother pulled him forward and that was that. Alexander never murmured so he was not checked. During the day he played as normal, rolling all over the floor when my mother chased him with a balloon and tickled him. He was fine. The burn was only discovered when he was having a bath. Alexander got in the water and then got out and when he turned round we saw a blister the size of a lady's small finger nail and it had gone pink around it about an inch. Alexander was not in any distress at all. He allowed my mother to attend to it and then he went to bed. He lay on his back to go to sleep.

No one can understand how Alexander did not feel the burn. A medical person has told me that there are fewer nerves in the place he burnt. If anyone burns their finger it is always painful because of all the nerves in a finger.

When my father returned Alexander to his father the following evening he explained what had happened. One week later, when it was another of our court hearings, everyone was 'up in arms' when we arrived. Simon had taken a photograph of the burn on an 8' X 4' sheet and it had obviously been 'doctored'. The burn was now black, twice the size and the pink was now purple. The solicitors and the legal guardian took the photograph to be genuine and I was to lose two nights and one day off one of my contact weekends and my parents were asked if they would have a geriatric assessment. My parents agreed and Simon was elated: He had a trump card. He had been trying to cut my contact down for a long time, especially my weekends, but when the solicitor told him that he would have to pay toward the cost of the extra work (about a thousand pounds) he decided he did not want to put my parents through the ordeal of having the legal guardian coming to my home to sit and watch how my parents were able to cope with Alexander and check on the safety of our home. My parents were also to have a medical examination.

The worst thing about the burn was that Simon and his partner both knew that it was not as bad as they were making it out to be.

Simon was too late with his withdrawal and my parents were to be assessed again. They had already had the legal guardian go to the rehab to see how his grandparents were treating Alexander as Simon had told her that they only took notice of me and not Alexander and that they didn't care about him. When the legal guardian went to the rehab she said she found no evidence of this. Alexander's grandparents love him and their other grandchildren dearly.

Simon had now started to ask for parental responsibility for his partner at court hearings as well as meetings so the judge said that if she wanted it then she had to go through the proper channels and apply through the court, filling in an application form for a residency order as she and Simon were not married and a residency order would allow her to get parental responsibility I was so upset. Alexander was my son and now I have to sit and let her take him over. It is all so wrong and I, because I am disabled, can do nothing about it. The whole battle for contact was throwing my recovery backwards. Some days when I received unpleasant letters I could do none of my exercises. I simply felt exhausted. I don't think my condition was taken into account by anyone.

The legal guardian was again checking on my parents' ability to look after Alexander and the safety of our home. She checked what actually happened when Alexander burnt himself. A normal person would accept that it was an accident, but not Simon. The legal guardian seemed to be satisfied with all she observed on her visits, so she stopped visiting.

Simon's partner was completely involved with my case now, as she had to fill in an application form for a residency order and make a statement. I was now up against two people in my fight for contact with Alexander.

In Simon's partner's statement she said that she did not realise what a selfish person I was; that I should be grateful to her because she had taken on the burden of looking after my son and also that I had no bond with him. I never wanted her to look after him; Alexander was my son and I wanted him.

I most certainly *did* have a bond, as did all of my family. When Alexander came on his contact day he would first run to his Nan and then he would say, "Mommy". My mother would have previously hidden me in one of the rooms, so she would say, "I don't know," and then Alexander would laughingly go from room to room saying "Mommy, No," until he found me and then I would get a kiss and a hug. He loved to sit on my lap and go shopping and to do cooking now that it was easier for him to reach the table. He would climb on my bed in the mornings and he also helped to feed me by pouring my food into the syringe and watching it go down "into Mommy's tummy")

Alexander was no burden to my family or me; my family make light of all situations so I live in a happy, mad house. When Alexander is here and his auntie, uncle and cousins come, it really *is* a mad house. The girls chase Alexander around and as Alexander is mad on *Spiderman*, Uncle Mark will walk him up the wall. I have had a lot of support from my mother's family. They have all spoilt Alexander with clothes and toys.

Simon's partner proudly said that she had looked after Alexander from April 2004 Three weeks after she had met Simon, he and Alexander had moved in with her yet she and Simon denied, right up until 2006, that they lived together. What was their reason for these lies? She had obviously forgotten that she had sent the police to my parents' home and also put legal documents on my parents' doorstep that had been delivered to her house for Simon. She maintained he did not live with her; this was in 2005-2006 so in my statement I told the court what she had done and also that she was a policewoman.

At one of my meetings my advocate was unable to attend as he had a prior engagement, so my mother sat with me. I found her to be a great help. Although my advocate was very good, he could only say the things I spelled out to him, whereas my mother, who knew my feelings, could voice my opinions for me. I had three of these meetings with my mother present and I think it helped my case greatly.

Simon and his partner sent to the court for a joint residency order and I felt sick at the thought that I was losing Alexander to them. Why could they not share Alexander with me? I was his mother, not her. All they would say was they wanted to be a family together, also what about her own sons? I think that the professionals were beginning to realise that Simon and his partner were trying to undermine me, which Simon denied. So they said that the residency order would have to be between all three of us, but as soon as Simon knew that I was to be included in the residency order, he got his partner to withdraw her application, as he said I was not to be included as it would undermine him. If that does not prove that he wanted me out of Alexander's life, I don't know what else would do it.

Simon's partner wanted to meet me and I was asked by the legal guardian if I would, but I refused and when Simon's partner wrote another statement she said that she could not understand why not as she had a good relationship with her ex-husband. Hello? Did her husband abandon her only a few months after she'd had his child which resulted in a severe stroke, just when he was needed the most? Then take her son and give him to another woman and then make her fight through court for the right to see him? I don't think so!

When I asked why she was so keen to meet me, as she had asked on a number of occasions, she said it was so that they could stand by me when we were at school so it would not be uncomfortable for them. I am in a wheelchair but I don't feel uncomfortable as I go to see my son. What planet is she on?

At another of my meetings with the legal guardian and Alexander's solicitor, I was asked to write Simon a letter to let him know how I felt about what my stroke had done to me but I must not blame Simon for anything in the letter. I think it was to see if they could get any form of reaction from him – perhaps to see if he had a heart. This is my letter, his reply and my letter to the legal guardian and Alexander's solicitor:

Simon,

I have set down in writing my feelings to see if you could try to understand just how I felt and still feel about my condition and situation. I am still sitting here in my wheelchair after nearly five years. I have some movement and can say a few words. As to be expected, my recovery is slow but I have a huge ache in my heart. I feel I am looked upon as having no feelings and am unimportant because I cannot express my feelings easily other than crying. I have a lot of feelings. I get very hurt. Really I want to scream, "I am me! I am Dawn! I am Alexander's mother!"

I struggle every day to try to improve myself, which will speed up with time. From when Alexander first came to see me in hospital in his incubator, I cried inside having to watch everything done for him by other people, things I wanted to do, I would have loved to have reached out and touched him, fed him and changed him and still long to do things for him but it is not to be. I think of all the care I have been denied giving him, but he makes me so happy when he reaches out, touches me and does things for me. Alexander accepts me as I am and I accept he needs looking after.

I never thought I would have such a maternal instinct as I have, from when I first saw him I loved him all 1lb 8oz of him. I feel I am being punished for having a stroke. I cannot say to people that I am Alexander's mother and I am not brain damaged, just because I am in a wheelchair and I cannot talk. I find this terribly frustrating having people talk over me and not to me. I want to people to try to understand me and have time to listen to me, it is very hard to be with a group of people and not be able to join in with their conversation and put my views over unless someone takes the time to use my letter board. I want to shout "hello, I am here, I am not Mrs Nobody". I will not come out of my stroke the way I went into it but I have a strong determination to recover. I can have a good life and I want a life with Alexander.

Simon, I have no animosity towards you or Maria for starting a new life together. It is what I expected you to do (albeit not as soon as you did). The one thing I would really like to know is why you changed so much? All I ask of you Simon is to share Alexander with me. He is my World.

Dawn

His reply:

Dawn,

I was supposed to not respond to your letter, isn't that the ridiculous situation we find ourselves in, we've allowed ourselves to be taken over by legal stupidity and seemed to have lost any ability to express our feelings due to perhaps being taken as a sign of weakness that will be reported to the court etc.

I'm not going to make any comparisons or even attempt to justify anything I've done. There is no point now but all I can say is that I truly feel terrible that you ended up how you did and I feel guilty for not being there for you or taking you somewhere else where they could have done something for you, but I can't change that now. You won't believe it but to some extent we were both victims. I felt alone and confused. Every day I would go to see Alexander without you, having to be told terrible things sometimes. I cried about what we had lost together, we shared everything, enjoyed the same things, the walks, visits to national trust places, holidays, music etc. I had to live in that haunted house, somehow the house changed without you, everything changed. Then in the middle of all this was the shining light, part of you and I - Alexander. I see us both in him and he will always have that. I wish things could have turned out differently but there are many *reasons why we are where we are today and the reasons are with both of us for that.*

I haven't changed really; I just cannot say anything whilst we are in this silly situation.

Anyway I know Alexander would accept you of course and I would never want to change that. I also want him to do the little boy things I was lucky enough to do so everything is a balance. It hurt when you said that I only wanted him for financial reasons, many fathers abandon their children – I never wanted to do that we just have to realise he has a life with both of us.

Simon

Letter to Solicitor and Legal guardian:

*Dear Mrs ****** and Mr *********

I opened up my thoughts to Simon; I would now like to open them up to you.

I mentioned in my letter how I cried inside because I could not do anything physically for Alexander. Can you imagine how I would feel watching Maria in my role as Alexander's mother?

I have always felt that Simon took Alexander away from me and gave him to Maria. When the P. R. was first mentioned when we were having a meeting with Simon in my house I crumbled, I then felt he really did want me out of the picture. For all the forgiveness I have given him over the last four years I cannot forgive him that. I feel it will take a lot of work and time before I could trust Simon again, he has so many times promised one thing then got cross and done another. If Simon meant half of his letter he would not keep trying to stop my contact at every opportunity he can.

I feel it would be very confusing for Alexander at his age for him to try to understand the situation and that he has to learn to spend short times with me. What could he or I gain from that, he would have no time to relax before he had to leave. The only people who would benefit would be Simon and Maria because they would have my weekends. I only have two mornings a month when Alexander can come onto my bed and relax with me. Alexander needs to have a fixed pattern of contact in which he is settled. But I would always help Simon out if he were unable to collect him from school.

If Simon starts to prove he is genuine then in time I would not feel too threatened. It is only now that Alexander has started school I have been fully involved in his progress and medical issues. Previously I had to give Mark Power of Attorney, so that I could get information about Alexander's health because I was being excluded.

My mistrust of Simon at the moment is great. I lived with him for fourteen years and he is not the same person I knew. His actions do not match his words.

I feel I cannot agree to be together at school for some time yet as that would create a false impression and I am not a false person. Alexander I am sure would feel the atmosphere and it would also make Alexander have to choose.

Let us all go along doing the very best for Alexander and aim to improve this with time. The conflict has to stop but realistically I do not have a great deal to say in the matter as Simon has Alexander.

Regards Dawn

I feel that Simon's letter in answer to mine was just lip service!!

Chapter 11

Although a lot of my time was taken up with making court appearances and writing letters I was also having appointments with my orthodontist who was trying to pull back my bottom teeth. I had one tooth taken out from the front to give room for my teeth to be pulled back. I had a brace put on which my lovely orthodontist would colour to match whatever colour I was wearing, then once my teeth had gone back I had a permanent wire fixed to the back of them and then I had a transparent retainer fitted over them. On my first visit after the retainer had been put on for three months the orthodontist and her assistant were over the moon that my teeth had stayed in place when the retainer was checked. They had been worried that the wire at the back would not hold them in place but it had, so hopefully my teeth will stay up. Apparently it is your lips that keep your teeth in place and as my bottom lip was so weak they had nothing to support them.

I had also been working hard on my degree and I am happy to say that I have passed my first two years of exams, one on Classical Studies and the other on Ancient Greek. I am now starting on my Latin course. When I take my exams, because I cannot go to any classes for them, I have an invigilator come to my house and sit with me while I do my exam. He only comes for three hours for two days and then because I am easily tired, I rest for two days. This is then repeated all over again as I have him sit for another two days and rest another two days then I have him sit for two hours on one day. I am then given two weeks unsupervised time. My unsupervised work is then calculated on my supervised time, which is a total of fifty hours. This would take other students three hours to complete but because I have to use my headset and I tire so easily I am given extra time.

As Alexander was now four years old and ready for school, he had to have an assessment done on him because he would need to have one-to-one attention at school. I had been waiting for Simon to organise it because all forms and appointments go to him, as he is the main carer. Simon did nothing about filling in the form to start Alexander's assessment and as it was getting close to Alexander starting school and Simon had decided to go on holiday, when asked about it I got my mother to phone the office of the assessment board and explain that I was concerned and asked if there was anything I could about it. The lady said if I emailed her she would accept that as authorisation as either parent could do it. Alexander's assessment went ahead and I am happy to say he was assigned thirty-two and a half hours one-to-one. Alexander started school in November 2007.

When the assessment board was processing Alexander's assessment I was sent a report from various people that were involved with Alexander. I then found out what had been said about me. Social Services wrote that Simon was the sole carer of Alexander because his wife did not live at the family home. The review date for this letter was 2006. Firstly I was *not* Simon's wife and secondly we had no family home because it had been sold. Another report was from the consultant paediatrician and he wrote I was brain damaged and could only understand if I was spoken to appropriately. I had to write to both to give them the true facts.

I was made to feel unimportant in Alexander's life as at one of the meetings I was told that the childminder was very significant in his life and she was asked to attend one of the future meetings. Then it was said that Simon partner's feelings had to be considered when it came to Mothers Day as she looked after Alexander she had already taught Alexander to call her mommy she said he had picked it up from her two sons. Do twenty-year-olds call their mother mommy? I was offered one hour for Mothers Day, after all what did I expect – I am only his mother!

The court hearing was coming to the final stages and Simon was resorting to desperate measures to try to reduce my contact with Alexander. The legal guardian had sent in her report on all the meetings she and Alexander's solicitor had had with my parents and me and Simon and his partner. When Simon read it (we are all given copies of all transactions) he was beside himself, as she basically saw no reason why my contact should not resume.

Simon disagreed with everything she wrote. He said her report was wrong that Alexander was not naughty at school as he had a report from the headmaster that contradicted hers. When the legal guardian spoke to the headmaster Alexander had not been at school long and had found it tiring as he was sent to school at quarter past eight in the morning until quarter to five and it was a little too much for him. Alexander had got so tired and naughty. But Simon's report was a more up-to-date one and Alexander had settled down quite a lot by then.

Simon said if the court let the legal guardian's report be presented in court then the court was corrupt. Simon also challenged my parents' medical report as he said the doctor had not been given the correct facts, that Alexander had had an accident at their house. Simon took the photos of the burn that he had made to look ten times worse than it was, to show my parents' GP. He said he was going to call the doctor and the headmaster as witnesses to disprove the legal guardian's report when he cross-examined her. The only thing I disagreed with in the guardian's report was that she said it was a tragedy on both sides; where was Simon's tragedy? All he had done was exchanged everything he had for another one, i.e. job, home and partner; and he also had Alexander, I lost everything I loved plus I am physically disabled and also had Alexander taken away from me.

When my parents were first asked to take a medical it was supposed to be a geriatric medical, but neither the legal guardian nor Alexander's solicitor could find one that was available. The judge said to Simon that if that was what he wanted my parents to have, then she would give him a week to find a doctor himself. If he could not, then my parents were to have only a normal medical examination but that did not satisfy Simon. After showing the doctor the photo, he asked for a letter. The doctor sent one to the court but it was not what Simon hoped for because she said that no medical advice was sought when the burn occurred which meant that Simon and his partner never thought it severe enough to have someone look at it. Also no scar tissue was found there. Simon's partner wrote to the court about the burn that as a police officer she has seen lesser injuries have more severe consequences (she wanted my parents clamped in irons) and that all everyone wants to do is give Alexander to a disabled mother and old-age pensioners. This woman is supposed to be a pillar of the community.

Simon also disagreed with a report written by the woman that deals with Alexander's hearing aids. She is a lovely person and she has been coming to see me for the past five years to keep me informed about Alexander's hearing and to show me any equipment that is new and they are going to try it on Alexander to help him. Now that Alexander is at school she sees him twice a week and Alexander is so used to her, he runs to her and puts his arms around her, yet Simon told the court she knows nothing about him and he 'rubbished' her report. He also said he would 'cross examine her'!

Chapter 12

Simon wrote some dreadful letters when the court hearing was pending. Once he wrote saying, what happens when my parents are no longer able to cope and I went in a home? I wrote back saying that I would only end up in a home if I was still married to him. My brother wrote a letter to show that he and his family would be there for me and that I would always have a home with them for Alexander. Simon wrote another letter that was so disrespectful to my parents that my solicitor when she received it was asked not to show it to me.

I had a couple of letters from Simon that I did not understand. One blamed my cousin for getting involved. Simon said we would have been OK if he had not. My cousin got involved because of Simon's behaviour toward me, the other woman he was living with and also because I asked him to help me to divorce Simon.

The other letter said that he and his family would always love me. How do I work that out? My mother left a message on Simon's father's answer machine to say it was a horrendous thing that had been done to me to have my baby baptized behind my back. I don't know if Simon's father had anything to do with it but his two daughters certainly did. I have never heard from them again. That was four and a half years ago and as far as Simon's love goes, the way he has treated me I don't think he knows the meaning of it.

I do have contact with Simon's mother and stepfather. They send me an M&S gift voucher every Christmas and also a letter letting me know how they are and I reply to let them know about Alexander and how I am progressing.

On the eighth of July I went to court for the final hearing. When we first arrived at nine a.m. (my mother and brother were with me as my father could not face any more) we were allocated a room to wait in while my barrister tried to get Simon to be reasonable. There was a lot of 'to-ing' and 'fro-ing' with my barrister saying, "It is like knocking your head against a brick wall when talking to Simon."

Simon and his partner were in another room. As the situation was not getting any easier the legal guardian, Alexander's solicitor and my barrister decided to go to see the judge. What was said there we will never know but at about twelve-thirty Alexander's solicitor came into our room and said if we would like to go home for our lunch, we could, and we were to be back for two p.m. My advocate went off shopping in Stafford although my mother did offer him some lunch at our house. We went home for a break.

We arrived back at the court at two p.m. and my advocate met us and told us that Simon, his partner and the legal representative, now occupied our room so as the restaurant was now closed to the public we were allowed to go and sit in there. My barrister came out after a while and said he had sorted everything out and showed Simon's proposals to me and my brother. Mark checked it over, picked something that was not quite fair, so back the barrister went and then he returned. He said Simon said "That's fine". I was being given more than I dared hope for, but less than I would like. What had happened while we were away? All through my court battle I had been told to not 'rock the boat'; keep Simon happy. I felt that whatever Simon and his partner wanted they got. But maybe this time things had gone my way for a change.

We were called into court to go before the judge. Simon was on his own as his partner had left to go to school to pick up my son. I went in with my advocate. We were in court for about thirty minutes. The judge commended both of us for coming to an agreement over our contact but said she did not want to see this case before her again. We left court to go home and celebrate.

My mind boggles at the legal system. They are the law and yet it seems as if their hands are tied when it comes to dealing with these mothers and fathers who use their children to get their own back on their partners. A child needs to have the right to know both parents as do the parents have the right to be a mother or father to their child unless there are extenuating circumstances.

Chapter 13

Now that my contact case is over I can put all my energy into trying to improve my body with the help of my physiotherapists and family. The physiotherapists are working me hard on my standing. I have now progressed to standing, with help, with a large Zimmer frame. When they first tried me standing with a normal-sized one it was way too small as I am five foot, then and a half inches tall and it made my bottom stick out, so they ordered another one, the tallest they could get.

I can now stand, unaided, for a minute. It's not long but it's a start. The joy I get from this is wonderful. Thank you, physiotherapists! My physiotherapists have lent me a Zimmer frame to bring home so that I can practice standing. When Alexander sees me being lifted onto my feet he says are you OK mommy and then he tells my parents to hold me tight. Alexander also tells everyone that mommy talks A, B, C.

When I think back to when I first went into hospital I am glad I am not a selfish person like Simon, because if I had been then when I first went into hospital and they wanted to operate on me straight away I would have let them. But a doctor came into my room and said, "Dawn, any day you can hang on to your baby will give him a better chance of living." I hung on for six days, saying, "I am fine," when asked how I felt, "except for the pain in my neck." The doctor thought I had just 'cricked' it then the doctors told me that things were getting serious and they would have to operate. I may never have had my stroke if I had been like Simon but when I look at my Alexander I am so proud and happy I gave him life.

As for me, I am continuing, albeit slowly, to make ripples.

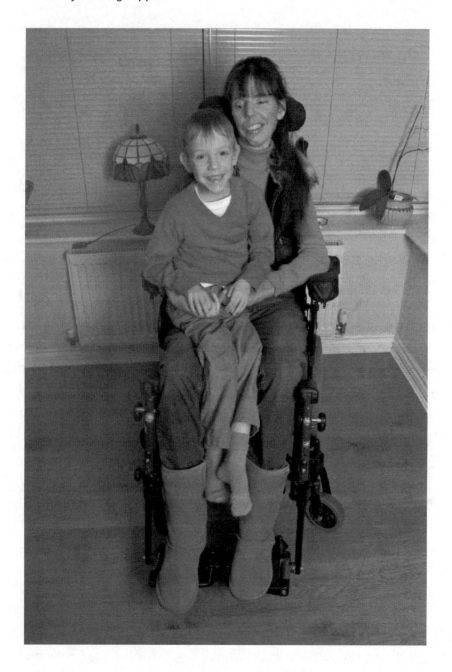

The End